"If you are in or entering the new w [barcode] ıd
you want to know everything about ɔy
Scott Billups. You'll be sorry if you
David Lynch—director

"An individualist in a town where conformity can be a Zen-like state of grace, Billups is not afraid to lock horns with mainstream studios as he seeks to invent "the new Hollywood."
Paula Parisi— *Wired* magazine

"Scott Billups is a twenty-first-century revival tent evangelist, but the story he's preaching has nothing to do with pearly gates, fire or brimstone. Scott is pushing the gospel of Silicon."
Craig McGillivray— *RES* magazine

"With this book Scott Billups has opened the Pandora's Box of moviemaking once and for all. He demystifies and simplifies the new digital paradigm as only a real expert can. Scott details with wit and passion how you can't be stopped if you really want to make a movie.... Between the pixels, digicams and cyberspace, herein lies real literature for a new millennium."
Philippe Mora—writer/director/producer

"A laid-back, self-taught, maestro of digital production, Billups is out on the cutting edge."
Buzz magazine—LA's Top 100 List

"Digital Moviemaking should be required reading for everyone from film-industry students to hardened movie moguls. It gives new perspective to the creative process of capturing the moving image, while focusing on aspiring filmmakers with 'credit-card budgets' who are challenging the status quo through digital technology."
Robert J. Estony, Director, Communications—Ikegami Electronics

MICHAEL WIESE PRODUCTIONS
www.mwp.com

Since 1981, Michael Wiese Productions has been dedicated to providing novice and seasoned filmmakers with vital information on all aspects of filmmaking and videomaking. We have published more than 50 books, used in over 500 film schools worldwide.

Our authors are successful industry professionals — they believe that the more knowledge and experience they share with others, the more high-quality films will be made. That's why they spend countless hours writing about the hard stuff: budgeting, financing, directing, marketing, and distribution. Many of our authors, including myself, are often invited to conduct filmmaking seminars around the world.

We truly hope that our publications, seminars, and consulting services will empower you to create enduring films that will last for generations to come.

We're here to help. Let us hear from you.

Sincerely,

Michael Wiese
Publisher, Filmmaker

THE FILMMAKER'S GUIDE TO THE 21ST CENTURY

DIGITAL

MOVIEMAKING

A BUTT-KICKING, PIXEL-TWISTING VISION OF

THE DIGITAL FUTURE AND HOW TO MAKE YOUR NEXT

MOVIE ON YOUR CREDIT CARD

SCOTT BILLUPS

Published by Michael Wiese Productions
11288 Ventura Blvd., Suite 821
Studio City, CA 91604 (818-379-8799) (818-986-3408 fax)
mw@mwp.com
www.mwp.com

Cover Design: Art Hotel
Book Layout: Gina Mansfield

Printed by McNaughton & Gunn, Inc., Saline, Michigan
Manufactured in the United States of America

ISBN 0-941188-30-2

Library of Congress Cataloging in Publication Data

Billups, Scott
    Digital Moviemaking: a Butt-Kicking, Pixel-Twisting Vision of the Digital
    Future and How to Make Your Next Movie on Your Credit Card / Scott Billups.

        p. cm.
        ISBN 0-941188-30-2
        I. Digital Moviemaking. II. Title.

                                                                        CIP

To

Warren Miller

For giving me my first paycheck in this industry
and for the example he has given us all as filmmakers

In Memory of

James Wong Howe

For teaching me to see light

TABLE OF CONTENTS

Chapter 5 - **TOOLS OF THE TRADE**

Chapter 6 - **DIGITAL CINEMATOGRAPHY**

Chapter 7 - DIGITAL CRAFTSMANSHIP

ACKNOWLEDGEMENTS

First, there is my fathomless appreciation of my wife Minky for maintaining an atmosphere conducive to non-stop writing and whose gravitational pull always seems to nudge me back into orbit.

My second acknowledgment would have to be to my long-time friend, and publisher, Michael Wiese. Without his guidance and patience, this book would be little more than hallucinated gibberish. To Brian McKernan, for fostering my literary endeavors for so many years, and to all the publishers of all the magazines who've published my ramblings.

A hearty tip-o'-the-hat to my good friend Steven Blumenfeld, who took time away from his hectic schedule to give the manuscript a technical hosing and to Tony Salgado, a comrade-in-arms in the never-ending battle to wrestle humanity from the binary equations of digital production.

Many thanks to my old friend and manager Paul Addis, who has succeeded in maintaining a work flow in the face of my overwhelming quest for adventure. To my long-suffering mentors Chuck Mellone, Lawrence and Ken Littleton, Stuart Volkow, Scott Auchmoody, Steve Lomas, Nick DeMartino, Mike Backes, Harry Marks, and all the other luminaries who have educated and inspired me.

I'm sure I speak for the greater community of digital moviemakers when I thank Mika Salmi, Gary Zeidenstein, the Algeri brothers, and my good friend Jeffrey Kramer for leading the online production community with such vision and integrity.

On the more corporate side, I'd like to thank Nolan Murdock at Panavision for his continuing support, even though I've probably caused far more damage to their equipment over the years than my meager business could ever pay for. And finally, to Sony, Panasonic, Ikegami, Canon, Apple, Adobe, Discreet Logic, Terran, and all the companies that make the tools that help us tell our stories.

FOREWORD
by
Roger Corman

Entertainment is entirely controlled by the populous. If it doesn't develop an audience it's gone. This is as true on the Net as it is with the big screen. Real talent is hard to fake. There are formulas and techniques that can help, but the really good stuff always shines through in the face of budgetary limitations.

The motion picture industry has always been an exclusionary affair. It takes lots of money to make a studio picture. Through the years Hollywood has created filters that let some people in and excludes others. Then along comes digital technology and the price point of entry becomes affordable to just about everyone. Hollywood reeled a bit but soon recovered by tightening up the filters. Then along comes the internet and the doors are swung akimbo.

Virtually anyone with an idea and a few bucks can now create a motion picture. In most cases the movie itself won't really go any-where, but the instantaneous presence that it generates within the industry is truly revolutionary. Sure there's a lot of bad cinema being made by this new cadre of digitally endowed moviemakers. What's new?

The future of cinema lies in the power of the pixel. The injection of fresh ideas and methodologies will only serve to mix up the metaphorical gene pool and empower a new generation of filmmakers.

With more channels of distribution there will be a greater demand for content, but less money to create it. The people who can create content the most cost-effectively will have a clear cut advantage. Heck, anyone can kick out a movie if you throw enough money around, but if you can tell a compelling story within the confines of a severely limited budget, then you're a true moviemaker and the future is yours to shape.

With more than 500 motion pictures to his credit Roger Corman is the hands-down, all-time, reigning king of moviemaking.

Noted for his keen ability to spot young talent, his most lasting legacy will undoubtedly be the legion of producers, directors, writers, and actors he has fostered, among them: Jack Nicholson, Francis Ford Coppola, Peter Bogdanovich, Martin Scorsese, Ron Howard, Joe Dante, James Cameron and the author of this book.

BINARY HORIZON

This is perhaps the easiest time in history to be successful. There is no other period in the time line of human endeavor when so many people have had the tools to do so much damage to the status quo.

ONLY HALF OF IT

You are only holding half of this book; the other half is online at (www.PixelMonger.com). As you progress through this book you will be guided to illustrations and given Web addresses that will allow you to reference the latest material in equipment, techniques, resolutions and formats. This unique combination of conventional and electronic publishing will give you a timely resource previously not possible.

You'll also have access to custom software applications, as well as downloadable and printable forms and templates that are capable of taking you all the way through the production of your movie.

Perhaps most importantly, you'll be guided to festivals and workshops, and hopefully the greater community of independent filmmakers. New distribution mechanisms are going online daily. No magazine, much less a book, could ever hope to guide you in these areas, but with the online aspect of this book, that's exactly what I hope to do.

My objective is to get you up and running as fast as possible. I'm sure there are those who will accuse this book of glossing over the technical details or spending too much time with peripheral politics. Truth is, you *don't* really need to know all the tweakie little nuances of this digital stuff. The beauty of technology is that success doesn't depend on whether or not you understand how it works; all you need to know is what it does.

And when you get to the end of your production, hopefully with the best-looking movie that your budget will allow, you'll actually have a clue as to what to do with it. To do that you'll need to have a decent understanding of the various industries involved and why they act the way they do. I've seen far too many aspiring artists stopped dead in their tracks because they lacked the most fundamental understanding of the real-world workings of the industry they were aspiring to join.

There are no brick walls, only seemingly impenetrable gaps in our understanding.

I've always found that Tokyo, Japan is perhaps the very best place to take the pulse of technology. Not so much the actual use of that technology, but rather the tempo of the bits and pieces that are marching toward us over the binary horizon. Like any large city, Tokyo is divided into numerous thematic regions that pander to the various aspects of the global human condition. My two favorite districts are Akihabara and Shinagawa.

Akihabara is the gizmo capital of the world. Imagine an electronics store from six years in the future that covers more than a square mile. Every storefront, every sidewalk, every alleyway, packed with a mind-numbing assortment of the guts of future technology.

I bought a 15" flat panel monitor from a street vendor, four years before they were even mentioned here in the U.S. My first ophthalmic quality virtual headset was purchased from a merchant I found deep within the bowels of a dark alleyway. Every square foot of this technological utopia is covered with stores and vendors both large and small, selling everything from bootleg chips to teleconference videophones.

Shinagawa, on the other hand, is the button-down yin to the haphazard yang of Akihabara. There's technology here all right, but it's not in plain view. Shinagawa is the heart of the global technocracy of image and sound, and the blood that curses through its veins is the hard currency of the world. I like to stay at a particular hotel there that overlooks a lovely pastoral park.

Across the street is a lovely tearoom complete with shoji screens and an ambiance of elegant industrialism. Off to the side of this ersatz tearoom is a rather formal lady sitting at a plain desk. Behind her stands a nondescript doorway that leads directly into the bowels of Sony corporate headquarters.

The first time Sony invited me for a visit was just after finishing my fully digital show called *A Day in the Life of Melrose Ave.* The idea was to shoot and edit a show entirely on the hard disk of a computer, and then take the computer to the television station, and broadcast it directly from the hard disk. An entire show created entirely within the digital domain and never touching videotape. Attempting that today is no big thing, a couple Fire Wire drives plugged into a laptop, but this was back in the early '90s, before the era of affordable gigabyte drives.

Well the show was fun but somewhat anti-climactic domestically because hardly anyone realized what had just been done. There was no reference or context, and as I've come to realize, technology without context is irrelevant. Not so with the Japanese. Within two weeks of

3

Digital production hasn't always been convenient, as this "location" shoot from the late 1980s illustrates.

wrapping production, I found myself sitting in the Sony tearoom. Upstairs, in this ultimate shrine to the next big thing, I discovered an endless procession of production environments that provide a razor-sharp oracle of what is around our collective corner.

Now keep in mind that I had been writing about digital film and video production technology for five of the leading industry magazines for more than six years. If anyone should have a clue about this stuff it should be me. What I saw completely blew my mind. How could I have been so blind to what was in the pipes? What I began to realize was that what we perceive as the bleeding edge of technology, even those of us writing about it, is only a carefully orchestrated ballet of illusions.

Once back from Japan, the digital camera concept became an obsession, every iteration getting smaller, with greater capacity and more resolution. The first truly luggable (as opposed to portable) camera system came off the benches in mid-1993. It took the RGB signal directly off the imaging chips and recorded it in compressed 8-bit; 4:1:1 to the hard drive using a prototype Video Explorer videographic board custom-made by my good friend and nerd savant, Brett Bilbrey. Since we were going for quality as opposed to quantity, the

drive could only hold 23 seconds of video at a time. Still, we used it on several jobs and kept on moving.

Yeah, I know its dorky-looking, but hey, it worked. Who'd have believed that in less than five years even better resolution would be available in a pocket-sized form-factor. Well, a couple weeks after the initial unveiling I found myself back in Japan, walking the hallowed halls of the undisputed leader in digital cameras, Ikegami. We basically talked about where we saw this

The Porta-Cam was dubbed by my friends as the first "luggable" digital camcorder. The batteries alone weighed more than 20 pounds.

5

whole thing going, I talking about the future of a low-cost digital camera with enough resolution to be blown up to film, while they talked of distribution mechanisms that allowed high-resolution video to be instantaneously shuttled around on a personal level. I tried not to smirk at their preposterous notions of global, broad-band communications.

I must've done something right because they let me borrow a digital camera head with a prototype imaging unit. They even supplied the chip schematics and wiring diagrams. My old friend Scott Achmoody stepped up to bat and made an even smaller and more powerful ITU-601 videographic board which we hot-wired into the camera's encoder, (sorry Ikegami) and created a working, digital camcorder. Okay, it wasn't the prettiest thing you ever saw but my SMPTE (Society of Motion Picture and Television Engineers) friends went nuts. Being a long-time SMPTE guy myself, that was enough for me. After several months of quasi-dependable performance, it was stolen.

A few years later I got a call from someone at the Academy of Television Arts & Sciences asking if I knew that Avid was campaigning for an Emmy. It seems they were under the impression that they had developed the digital camcorder. They'd taken the same camera head (now called the HL-76), updated the same basic design and called it the CamCutter. I reminded

The Digi-Cam wasn't very pretty but its images were. The first true 601 camcorder that wasn't under a cloak of corporate secrecy gave semi-dependable service for almost a year. It was used on several commercials, music videos and an infomercial.

them that there was a very nice article in the August '93 issue of their own *Emmy* Magazine, with a lovely picture of me standing there holding my home-made digital camcorder that pre-dated the Avid claim by more than two years. Never really heard much about it after that.

But I did get invited back to Japan. This time, to give a presentation on digital production techniques at Matsushita (Panasonic). So there I was, back in Shinagawa, where they put me up at the same hotel I had stayed at when I was visiting Sony; what a coincidence. I had sent a bunch of projects that I'd been working on over to them several months before so they could "process" them. I wasn't really sure what "process" meant but I figured that whatever it was, it wasn't going to hurt the resolution. The car shows up, I hop in and a few seconds later they let me off in front of a rather nondescript building. From what I can tell, it's just around the block from Sony.

The total absence of technology is what hit me first, and the enormous pyramidal vault of the interior. Easily ten stories high, each floor's concentricity is smaller than the last. After a few seconds you adjust to the shear dynamics of the lobby's volume as you're hit with the soothing sounds of a babbling mountain stream.

There, on the lobby floor, meandering through hundreds of tons of perfect granite rocks and boulders, was a perfect mountain stream. With trout! Gotta tell ya', I'm a pretty ardent fly fisherman, and this place had me going. An enormous Sequoia was lying on its side, its top-most surface hewn and polished to the perfect definition of wood. Off to the left the stream passed before the entrance to a cave, apparently created by the random collision of several house-sized boulders in some theoretical cataclysm.

7

A tiny wooden bridge gently arched over the stream allowing access to the enigmatic cavern. As I set foot among the mighty boulders I was guided through a few twists and turns before entering the most hi-tech theater environment in the world. They had up-converted everything that I had sent them into their "HiVision" (Hi-Def) format and handed me a little controller that would transmit my "processed" video images directly to their HiVision satellite, along with the live camera shot of my presentation. The resultant multi-stream signal could then be mixed in real time at any of the six locations that were receiving it. At each location it was being projected onto an 18 x 32-foot electronic theater screen. This was back in 1994.

I'm not invited to Japan because I'm such a smarmy good guy and they just love my company. They haul my shaggy butt over there and give me access to nifty new toys because I do unconventional things with their technology, and because I create content. These are the two commodities that the Japanese have the least of, and value most. It is a relationship of mutual carnality, although I imagine the spigot will tighten after this book makes its rounds.

The point I'm trying to make is that whatever hype or digital palaver you've been buying into, well, just don't buy into it too deeply. The man behind the curtain is Japanese and personally I'm very, very glad. Unlike the crew that runs Hollywood, the Japanese are hard but ethical businesspeople who constantly exhibit strong moral character. Society can absorb only so much technology at a time without killing itself off or re-igniting the Luddite rebellion.

Just imagine if the greedy, soulless mothers in Hollywood actually had a say in matters. They'd glut the market, take their booty and retire in a heartbeat. You know it, I know it and they know it. Hollywood is a metaphor that has finally outlived its usefulness. The only studio even somewhat dedicated to advancing the technology of cinema is Sony. No one else is even close. Ever hear of the Paramount Studios Hi-Def Center, or the Warner Bros. Image Works?

The flow of technology is strictly regulated. It's a good thing. Get used to it.

So, what does this mean to our time line of broad-band digital movies, or film resolution cameras? Silicon, the relentless equalizer, has empowered a new generation of filmmakers by releasing them from the shackles of burgeoning budgets. The enviable result of this rampant technogogary is re-emergence of the professional generalist — one person, armed with the power of silicon who can perform the job of many. While budgets fall in the face of innovation, so unfortunately does the craft of cinema suffer too. By simply allowing more people access to the tools of the trade we are creating a vast glut of mediocrity.

Not that the studios don't kick out the mindless piece of crap on a regular basis. The difference is people still pay to see their big-budget, mindless pieces of crap.

You, however, as an independent filmmaker must deal with an extremely large mechanism that is deeply vested in propagating an endless stream of festival fare. Kind of like spreading manure on your strawberry field. Spread enough of it and pretty soon something sweet's going to start popping up.

The fact that there are a lot of bad movies getting made is really a good thing. It means that the tools are becoming more accessible. Look at any other form of expression — painting, sculpting or writing for example. Everyone has access to the tools of creation.

Everyone has the ability to put some words to paper, or pixels to liquid crystal as the case may be. A lot of people give it a shot and nothing happens. Doesn't necessarily mean that their words are less valuable. As the tools become affordable, the craft becomes an art form. Art is very democratic.

Virtually any contemporary home computer has the capacity to create a movie. Movies are becoming as ubiquitous as pencils. In a few years your personal movie will become the equivalent of a calling card, your statement of who you are and what you believe. People will drop in to your site, watch your movie and get a pretty good idea of what you're up to.

Perhaps you've key-worded it so it shows up in a broad spectrum of search engines. People start migrating to your MooV and realize that you've actually got something different to say, or the way you say something common finally makes sense to them. That's the trick, you know — taking an aspect of someone's life and creating a fresh perspective on it. You figure out how to do that on a dependable basis and you've got a fan for life.

Then one day some guy with a co-opted, time-share satellite feed sees your movie and links it to a friend in London, who agrees that it has a certain commercial merit to it. They offer to set up a theatrical exhibition and you agree. The online hype machine starts churning out PR and sending even more clips of your movie to the numerous venue sites. And finally, when your pixels hit the screen, the crowd goes wild. What's not to like?

Online exhibition is already a popular alternative release mechanism for both low- and high-resolution moviemakers. Every studio, every network, every Tom, Dick, and Scotty has a personal Web site dedicated to seriously denting the status quo, and the process is only going to get faster. And when will the technology arrive that enables this digital utopia of content? Why funny you should ask. It's already here. Actually been here for quite a while.

And when will we see movies broadcast from satellites, directly into theaters? Seven years ago. When will we see film resolution motion picture cameras? Five years ago. Sony already has one, Panasonic too. When do we get to play? Aha, now that's the real question.

THE WORM TURNS

Time was when film grain meant you were watching a quality story. Generations of kids grew up accepting the cinematic nuance of film as a qualitative Holy Grail. Today's market grew up on the luminous images of video and computer games. Grain doesn't hold as much subliminal impact for them. Before this book goes into its second edition, people will be downloading movies and playing them on hand-held devices. As much as we might like to believe that the large cinema screen represents the pinnacle of success, it is access, more than size, that will drive this industry into the future.

What we sacrifice for the crisp pictures and clear sound of the new generation of digital films is the subtle richness and full spectrum of emotion that the projected film medium provides. It is simply harder to be swept away by a tiny image.

The question is, "Will the audience notice?" That's all that really matters. I've spent my life behind film cameras. I can field, strip and clean a Mitchell Mark II in a swamp at midnight and come away with a clean gate. If anyone's gonna give you a negative report, it'd be some crusty ole curmudgeon like me. But I can't. I'd actually like to, but I just can't.

Digital isn't film; it won't be for years to come. What it does deliver is a far more efficient method to produce and distribute motion pictures. Shows like *The Blair Witch Project* stand as a testament that resolution isn't nearly as important as a good story line. If you keep the audience involved, they will forgive just about anything.

Bottom line, digital projections are generally better for everyone. The inherent resolution and image quality of a well-projected digital image in many instances surpasses a majority of film projections. Industry pundits will try to argue resolution and color-space issues, and to a certain extent they have a point. Fact is, if you follow the basic tenets of this book, your project, even if it's an ultra-low budget affair, will have the potential to compete with studio productions. And this, my friend, is where the solid human waste hits the air re-circulation device.

THE POLITICALLY INCORRECT VIEW

The reason it is so damn hard to break into the film business is that it is a tightly controlled industry. Always has been. To succeed you must understand how the industry works. To do that we must step, ever-so-lightly outside the bounds of political correctness.

A hundred years ago the film industry was dealing with a dramatic evolution in both technique and methodology. The structure that the movie industry adapted was based on the work of some of this country's most respected original thinkers. Thomas Edison, Henry Ford, and others created an environment of such efficiency that Hollywood has never again accomplished so much with so few, for so little.

Problem was, their formula presumed that each person in the process was highly proficient in the profession, and further presumed that each person possessed a "civilized person's sense of ethics."

Gradually, as more and more nonessential personnel infiltrated the studio system, it began to buckle from inexperience and graft. Nepotism became standard practice, and with it came ethnic polarization and the inevitable decline in the cost-effectiveness of the production process itself.

Today we are faced with the same set of circumstances that filmmakers of the last turn of the century had to face. The current need for adaptation to digital technologies is the same kind of situation that the studio system dealt with back in 1902.

The problem lies in the fact that we have no direction today. There are no outstanding leaders in the field of technology and innovation. We have become a corporate village, where original thinkers are absorbed into the contextual womb of the enterprise. Then along comes the cultural Cuisinart. The Net is the great equalizer.

Not that the studios aren't trying their damndest to get their claws around it as well. Problem is, the only content they have to supply the global Internet community is reconstituted offerings from their aging catalogues. The Net however, is democratic; it only rewards effort, not "connections." The fact that your uncle has a powerful Web site will not guarantee *your* success.

The same people who control the film business control virtually all media in this country including television and newspapers. Everything you read, hear or see via the popular channels of media distribution in this country is controlled in some way by these same few people. They have an almost neurotic preoccupation with keeping the balance of opinion subtly weighted in their favor.

Since you are now guilty of bucking their system, don't count on popular media to promote your project. If by some outside chance your project picks up momentum and becomes financially viable, don't worry, they'll find you.

The important thing to realize here is the difference between empowerment and enablement. Low-cost video production environments have been with us for a while, and the sophisticated up-conversion algorithms that allow us to turn the video image into a frame of film have been around since the '80s. Video filmmakers have been enabled for some time; however, it's only recently, due to technological leaps in the Internet, that videographers have been empowered to become filmmakers.

Because of the Internet, everyone has an equal opportunity to succeed or fail based on the quality or commerciality of his or her project. This democratization of the channels of communication is a dangerous thing to an industry so heavily vested in maintaining a pseudo-reality. As hard as they try, the people who run the media can't get a foothold on the Internet. It moves too fast for organizations that are so lumbering and slow-witted.

The Time-Warner/Yahoo deal got a lot of press and airtime because they own the presses and control the airways. Time-Warner saw AOL as its salvation for being so late in entering into the electronic age, while AOL saw Time-Warner as the great bastion of the content it so desperately needs.

What AOL failed to realize is that re-purposing pre-existing content doesn't work; the early days of CD-ROMs already proved that. Digitizing a bunch of old re-runs and movies, and offering them online is, quite simply, simple minded.

What Time-Warner will inevitably discover is that AOL's closed system is an aging metaphor that will pass into insignificance, as an increasingly savvy consumer base sets up virtual residency in the online land rush.

The name of the game is content. C. O. N. T. E. N. T. Anyone who has an urge to dive into the pixelated pool of digital production should have it tattooed to the inside of their eyelids. Anything that you create, regardless of whether you call it a digital movie or online enter-tainment, is content. We've got an entirely new environment here, with new rules and new opportunities. The infertile mind sees this merely as a way to combine existing environments, rather than recognizing it as the entirely new communications modality that it truly is.

The studios talk of "generating new revenue streams" rather than of fostering new experiences; "eyeballs" rather than minds. If you approach the Internet as just a way to make some money, all you'll end up doing is making money. Hey, maybe one of those megalomaniacal companies will buy you in the misguided belief that they can actually own content.

If, however, you approach it as a way to enrich people's lives by creating content that speaks to the essence of their humanity, you'll be con-tributing to an entirely new communications paradigm that has the potential to change the time line of human endeavor. Oh yeah, and you'll end up making lots of money.

15

The studios are all actively trying to get involved by re-purposing pre-existing catalogues. Sorry, guys. Shovel-ware doesn't work, but then aging content is all they've got left. They can't actually make anything anymore because they got out of the business. See, the studios no longer make movies. They make deals, and serve as a hub for numerous "mini-majors" who generally further subcontract to production companies (my own Electric Sandbox Productions is one), who then hire freelancers to augment their own in-house staff. In the "big five" major studios there are probably less than a few thousand employees. In essence, the studios themselves are little more than real estate and equipment rental facilities.

In a way, a movie studio is the ultimate metaphor for the Net. A central hub connecting smaller, more mobile versions of itself that, in turn, rely on numerous smaller independent companies to actually create content. Problem is, new distribution mechanisms start at the bottom and don't need the top. The feet simply disconnect from the rest of the body and walk away.

The new generation of studios will be online — more a group of people who agree upon a common set of digital standards than a physical environment. The new studio is unencumbered by the need to maintain a physical property and the obligatory staff of lawyers and MBAs. By virtue of its virtuality, the new studio is a high-density mix of production people and creatives. With increased efficiency comes increased economy. The ability to collaborate globally has opened the very process of production to the point where virtually every significant motion picture in the last several years was created outside Hollywood.

And when it finally comes time to release your movie, online distribution mechanisms will continue to reinvent the industry on a daily basis.

And what of the conventional movie theater? It is quite simply a dinosaur, little more than a human petri dish, an excuse for something to do on a date. Unless you're lucky enough to catch a movie in its first dozen or so showings, you're watching something that has far less image quality than a good digital projection. Even at the first screening of a major motion picture, you're sitting there watching an image that's five or six generations away from the original camera master.

There is an enormous investment here in film projection technology. Our media moguls have a vested interest in maintaining the status quo. In their favor is the fact that digital projections are only 4:1:1 (we'll get to that in a later chapter), but that will change; and when it does, their house of cards will fall.

All of the analog links in the digital chain of communication are destined to fail as the Net continues to connect all things. We are lurching inexorably toward an all-digital cinema in which film-quality images will be recorded onto hard drives, edited and manipulated on digital editing equipment, beamed to a satellite and projected digitally into a theater (or headset) near you.

Right off the top the studios stand to save more than $200,000,000 a year in duplication and shipping alone (the math: 3,825 theaters x $3,000 per print (which is only good for 4 weeks) x 13.5 (number of 4-week units in a year) = $154,912,500). Add to that the estimated $47,000,000 in shipping costs, and there are some serious savings. Kodak estimates a 1.4 billion-dollar savings worldwide — sobering numbers from the leading supplier of film.

There are, of course, the obvious standardization issues, copyright infringement, intellectual property and the like. These are merely grist for the lawyers, who always swarm around innovation. So if the technology's here, why haven't we seen an overnight switch to digital projection? Like almost all technological innovation, society can only absorb so much at a time. Since technology isn't hindered by the inadequacies of the human brain, there is a vast bottleneck of innovation just waiting to be unleashed. It's already here. It already works.

Point is, there's never been a better time to break into the movie industry. The price point of entry is affordable to everyone and the access to alternative distribution methods has never been more democratic. Doesn't matter what nationality or religion you are or where you live, you've got an equal opportunity to make a total ass of yourself.

I am constantly amazed at the unqualified freedom that we possess as filmmakers. This is the only country in the world where the motion picture industry isn't regulated by the government — the only place your script doesn't have to be submitted to a federal review process. Take advantage of this unprecedented freedom.

And if, by some idle muse from the cosmos, your film has merit, the studios will find *you*. After waiting around for a year or two, they might throw a few million into advertising and ship your little movie out to theaters. Yawn.

COLD AS ICE

As a moviemaker you're now part of the ICE business. Information, Communications, and Entertainment — and everything you create needs to connect. Movies need to be designed from scratch to be malleable to a wide variety of applications. To paraphrase from Kevin Kelly's book *New Rules for the New Economy*, "The more connections your content makes, the more valuable it becomes."

We have become a Net-based economy and the coin of the realm is content. Think of your movie as value. By freely distributing pieces of that value, you will feed the Web, and the return on your investment will be compounded daily. Don't have enough cash to finance your whole project? Make a good trailer and get it out there. The more aspects of your project you can tie to the Net, the greater your return on investment will be.

Content is power in the new Net economy. Whatever form movies take from here on out, the more connectability they have; the more inherent resources packaged with a film, the more valuable it becomes. By allowing your movie to interact with a networked community (the Internet) the value of that community increases exponentially as you join. That's the beauty of digital production. While the studios blunder along dropping pennies into the cookie jar, your digital contribution is earning compound interest.

Think of the Net as a hub of opportunity. The ultimate expression of free enterprise. Every festival you're in, every Web cinema site that runs a clip, every online critic that offers his or her opinion just makes you and your movie that much more connected. As your movie interacts with various nodes, it acquires the inherent value and inertia of those sites. On the Web, everyone is looking at everything. A festival chairperson may have previously caught an early sample of your work while browsing one of the many cinema Web sites.

Relationships on the Net are often more intimate and economically involved than conventional acquaintances. They may find your submission to their festival a "no brainer"; after all, you've already been introduced. They've already invested online time in downloading your preview, and everyone likes to see personal investments flourish.

By pre-involving people in your project you ensure multiple channels of opportunity for yourself. Your movie is merely the immediate beneficiary. The real issues reside with you as an independent film-maker. You're reading this book, you're reading articles, surfing the Web, snooping around, getting ready to make your first movie. Cool. So do it already. Even if it's a wretched, bloated, speed bump of crap. So maybe your second one will be better.

Don't worry about lack of budget. Your first several projects are going to be an eternal source of embarrassment anyway. Don't obsess about printing to film; in many cases it is neither necessary nor warranted. The important thing to do is keep shooting. As soon as you're done with one project, get involved with another.

The future lies with you, the digital filmmaker, not with Hollywood. It's really just as simple as that. Don't worry about Tinseltown; it's just a place where people go to make deals, not movies. Its only contribution to the GNP is banal sitcoms and anemic award shows that try in vain to propagate their ragged myth. They've got their little clubs and clans, and unless you know the secret handshake you don't stand a chance. The puddle has dried up and all the slimy little tadpoles are gasping for air. Hollywood has quite simply regulated itself out of business.

If you've got the inspiration and the energy, and still have enough leverage on your Master Card for a camera and a computer, you're Hollywood. Wherever you're standing is the production capital of the world. If nothing else in this book sticks, don't lose that thought.

CAST 'N' CREW

Who does what and why, and how technology allows different jobs to collapse and combine.

One of my favorite quotes regarding technology's effect on the conventional production paradigm is from Dr. Eric Martin, Associate Dean at the California Institute of the Arts, in Los Angeles:

> We're on the lip of an abyss... all media formats are collapsing quickly into one common digital language...*The most valuable worker is the one who can combine previously separate skills creatively...* it means the revalidation of the professional generalist as opposed to the professional specialist. In a few short years, it's possible that low-cost desktop systems will provide the equivalent to conventional sophisticated production environments. The premium becomes not who has the tools but rather who has the ideas.

As much as you might like to think of yourself as the lone desperado out there shooting away, its almost impossible to create anything of lasting value in a vacuum. Moviemaking is a process that involves alternative points of view. Controversy stimulates creativity and without it you become stagnant. No matter how blindingly brilliant you think your idea is, no matter how proficient you think you are at the craft of cinematic, one-way narrative, motion picture production is the most collaborative of art forms.

Many of the various jobs in the process require a variety of both right and left hemisphere functions. It is very difficult to transition from the mindset of budgetary concerns to the mindset of writing a line of dialogue or setting a shot.

The writer who rejects the cliché and creates characters who constantly evolve and engage the audience's deepest, unresolved emotions will always find more than a fair share of success.

The director who allows the actor be in the moment, thinking real thoughts and feeling real feelings right in front of us, will connect to the audience in a way that will seem magical.

The cinematographer who uses light to paint the spectrum of emotions across the palette of the human face will bring life and vitality to the characters.

The producer who makes good choices, picks good people and then gets out of the way of telling the story will be financially rewarded.

What are your goals and objectives? What inspires you? Scrutinize your motives. Do you have a passion for storytelling? Are you drawn to celebrity? Are you merely fascinated by the technology? Do you love working with other talented, passionate people toward a collective goal, or are you just looking for a good way to get laid?

Many successful actors are quite simply people in search of a per-sonality. Many directors are little more than opinionated control freaks. A vast majority of industry personnel embrace the production crew as a surrogate family. As many people as there are in this glorious industry, there are an equal number of motivations.

The trick, the secret, is not in following your dreams but rather in following your proclivities. The dark alleyways of Hollywood Boulevard are full of dreamers who let the easy flow of brash opinion cloud the subtle gift of inspiration.

You may be drawn inexorably by the creative outlet that cinema provides. I know that it's been my single biggest drive, though I do occasionally get sidetracked by the irresistible lure of technological innovation.

Like a great painting by a true master, the cinema combines a duality that spans the spectrum of the human condition. From the greedy lawyers to the gregarious gaffers and grips, this industry embodies the most robust assortment of characters found anywhere. The secret lies in finding your natural place within the process.

GET A GRIP

First thing to do is ask yourself, what do you see yourself doing? What are your goals and objectives? Sure, it's your idea and probably even your script, but are you really the best person to direct or shoot it? Maybe since you have "the big picture," the project would be far more successful if you acted as Executive Producer or let someone else take a pass at that "gem" of a script. It's great if you enjoy making movies, but if your project doesn't make money, or you don't pay back the people who invested in your project, your future as a moviemaker is going to be severely limited.

Perhaps the single best way to make sure that your production is successful is to get people who have the temperament for each job function to perform those jobs. There are a dozen major job descriptions in the moviemaking process and each is responsible for dozens of underlying departments. Each of these departments breaks down and branches out to tens if not hundreds more job titles, given the size of the budget.

On projects with severely limited budgets many of these jobs can be combined, allowing a single person to wear multiple hats. The problems start when, in the name of budgetary limitations, one of these jobs is eliminated rather than absorbed. The resulting hole in your organization can sink your project before it's even had a chance to leave the dock.

THE PROCESS

Starting from the point of view of a conventional, moderately budgeted, 35mm motion picture production, and continuing on down to the ultra-low budget "Lone Wolf" video project, let's take a look at what the various jobs do and why they're so important.

There are numerous ways to break down the motion-picture hierarchy — Studio Boss, Executive Producer, Director, Writer, and so on in a linear fashion. The problem is that the organization of a motion picture isn't linear and not all people are around for the duration.

A writer is actively involved at the start of a project, many times even before a director has been attached. The editor, who in many ways has the final word, may not even know of the project until principal photography has been finished. But, generally the writer hangs around on the periphery, sometimes contractually obligated to generate the occasional script fix, and editors generally cruise into the dailies just to get an idea of what's going on.

The production process can also be broken down into the distinct stages of DEVELOPMENT, PREPRODUCTION, PRODUCTION, POSTPRODUCTION, and DISTRIBUTION. Various job functions span all five stages, while some deal with only one or two stages in the production process.

> • DEVELOPMENT: This is the period in which the initial concept, whether for a motion picture or television show, is conceptualized, written and pitched, though not necessarily in that order. You could find yourself pitching a hairball concept or a full-blown script. You could be pitching for the $500 you need to bail your cameraman out of jail or twenty million dollars to make your next science fiction extravaganza. Once you've convinced someone to back your cinematic venture you've got to let all the good people who just anted up to have their way with you. Don't take it personally; it's just the way they do it here in Hollywood.

> • PREPRODUCTION: You've got your money, the scabs are healing up nicely and you're slamming together cast and crew, trying desperately to find a production facility out of the country so you can get away from all these studio creeps. This is when the project takes on its timbre as the cast and crew become the woof and weave of the story's tapestry. Mistakes and shortcuts here will, quite literally, haunt you till the day you die.

• PRODUCTION: "Lights, Camera, Action!" Once you're rolling, the sheer inertia of the process begins to sink in. The train has pulled out of the station and it's a whole lot longer than you imagined. Every decision that you've made up to this point is now following you down the track and will continue to do so until you utter the final "Cut, it's a wrap."

• POSTPRODUCTION: A lot of production people look at this as their time to come up for a breath of fresh air. It is technically the end of the initial manufacturing process. If you're a director or other heavily vested individual, you're swimming toward the surface like everyone else; but just before you break through, the editor, who's got these really big lungs full of fresh air, grabs you by the ankles and drags you back down.

If the production process could be described as running around a cactus patch in bare feet, trying to stomp out small fires, the postproduction process could be described as an endless, featureless exercise in cave dwelling. Every mistake you've made, every bit of coverage you didn't get, every time you said "We'll fix it in post," this is when it all comes back to haunt you. And your loyal cast and crew? They've all gone on lovely vacations, hanging out on beaches, and sipping margaritas. And you? You're sucking down two-day-old coffee in a building that should have been condemned at the last turn of the century, trying to figure out a polite way to ask your editor to increase his personal hygiene regime to twice a week.

• DISTRIBUTION: Damn, just when all the wounds had healed from the development process, here come a whole new herd of bison intent on having their way with you. They're called distributors, syndicators and network executives — and every one of them thinks you've got a purdy mouth. If you're really lucky, and the distributors like your movie, these beasts will set your movie up for exhibition; and if you're really, really lucky, the audiences won't hate it.

Then one day the check clears the bank, you're out on the promo circuit, and all you can think about is gettin' back in there and doin' it all over again.

I guess I should apologize for my cavalier and somewhat jaded view of the time-honored process. Those who have yet to make their first sojourn into the bowels of the Hollywood machine might find my observations rather crude. Hey, write your own book.

WHO DOES WHAT

In the most typical industry parlance there is a dividing line of job functions in the production process. It is called, quite simply, THE LINE. You're either above it or below it. I like to think of all of the people above the line as the people who don't get their hands dirty, while the people below the line are the ones who actually make the movie. So, above the line you've got all the producers, writers, the director, and the actors, while below the line hover all of the production staff and assistants to everyone above the line.

The basic rule of thumb is that the Producer hires everyone above the line while the UPM (Unit Production Manager) hires everyone below the line. Think of a Unit Production Manager as the below-the-line producer, or in military terms, the staff sergeant. Simply put, they run the show. The job is one of the hardest, most important and least appreciated, because it is a full-time battle to maintain a creative atmosphere in an environment that all too easily gets bogged down in technical minutia.

There is a growing trend to call Production Managers, Associate Producers, which to me is somewhat akin to calling DaVinci a paint slinger. But hey, I guess when you're standing at a bar, trying to impress the hot blond that just walked in, it sounds a lot cooler to say you're a Producer than a Unit Production Manager.

So basically the UPM takes the script and develops the first budget that anyone really pays any attention to. He also figures out how many days the project should take to shoot, and between two factors, Time and Money, calculates the Production Value. Basically the UPM negotiates a formula as old as production. Price, Quality, or Speed, pick any two.

The Directors Guild of America takes a much more succinct view of the UPM's functions, essentially stating:

> The Unit Production Manager, under the supervision
> of the Employer, is required to coordinate, facilitate
> and oversee the preparation of the production unit or
> units assigned to him, all off-set logistics, day-to-day
> production decisions, locations, budget schedules
> and personnel.

Of all the people involved in each of the five distinct processes of production, the UPM is one of the most important job functions. In many instances, a good UPM is far more important than a competent director. Second in importance to the UPM is the First Assistant Director, who actually does all the paperwork that keeps the production humming along.

There are two things a production runs on, vast amounts of paperwork and junk food. In my years of production experience, I can't remember a craft service table that didn't have a half-empty canister of Twizzlers sitting on it. But I digress. So the First AD is basically responsible for breakdowns and preparing the stripboard, the shooting schedules, day-out-of-day schedules, cast availability, call sheets, and weather reports, and is occasionally required to direct background scenes and supervise and direct crowd control.

While the First AD is doing all this work, the Line Producer is busy dealing with emergencies and trying to keep the show running while also trying to take credit for everything the UPM does.

A good Director is essentially "an allower." He comes on the set every day and allows everyone to do his or her job. More often than not, he's had little, if anything, to do with the script and almost nothing to do with securing financing, other than lending the credibility or infamy of his name to the process. Hopefully the Director is an inherently good storyteller and is capable of guiding the collective consciousness of the audience.

Directors are essentially the keepers of the metronome by which the process evolves. It is their responsibility to translate the script into visual terms. Hopefully the Producers hired a good Casting Director who picked good Actors who personify the roles. Then all that is left is for the Director to put them in the right places so they can do what they were hired to do.

29

Far more important to the look and feel of the movie is the DP (Director of Photography). For many years it was the Cinematographer who ran the production. It was only when the ASC (American Society of Cinematographers) went up against the far superior cunning of the DGA (Directors Guild of America) that the Director emerged as the on-set boss.

For the Director it often is the first day on the job, while the Cinematographer, more with film than video, needs to have a life-time of experience. The DP relies on a staff of Gaffers and Electricians to move lights and direct and modify the beams they throw. The Best Boy assists the Gaffer in setting up the lights, while the Electricians make all the necessary electrical connections and maintain the power supply.

One of the more notoriously gregarious members of the production crew are the Grips. Basically, for anything, other than lights, that needs to be moved, one of these guys "grip" it and move it. They are the handymen of the set, building scaffolding, placing props and creating unique devices to assist in various shots. If the camera is set on a dolly, it's the Dolly Grip who physically moves it.

In film productions and higher-end video productions, the audio is recorded separately from the image. The Sound Recordist (Sound Man even if they're female) and the Boom Operator are responsible for recording not only the spoken sounds of the actors, but also a catalogue of ambient "room" sounds that will be used later by the editorial staff.

The Script Supervisor is essentially the Director's brain. Rarely, if ever, are the scenes in a movie shot in sequential order. It is the

Script Supervisor who is responsible for making sure that everything from clothes and hairdos to the position of the dead body matches the shot done at another time. This person is also responsible for making sure that all the scenes have been shot from all the necessary scripted angles.

Second Unit does stunts, effects shots, crowd scenes, battle scenes, and generally shoots all the plates for later effects shots if there isn't a dedicated effects unit on the show.

At the very bottom of the heap are the lowest-paid employees, the PAs (Production Assistants), otherwise known as gophers (go for this, go for that). Their job is to direct traffic, control access to the set and go for stuff.

So that's a rather basic, albeit tongue-in-cheek, overview of the essential structure of your basic motion picture. Figure an average $10 million project will have a couple hundred people running around between several stages and locations. But hey, you don't have $10 million. That's why you're reading this book.

So now we gotta figure out how you can cram all those job descriptions into three or four people. First thing you've got to do is figure out who the most important people are. Simple. Unit Production Manager, Cinematographer, Grip. That's it. Notice that the Director didn't make the cut. As dramatic as it may sound, the Director just isn't that important to real production methodology. So here's how we're going to combine the jobs.

- DEVELOPMENT: Like the slimy caterpillar that is destined to evolve into a beautiful butterfly, the UPM starts out as an Executive Producer. He is like an organ grinder who, along with his trained monkey (Cinematographer/Director) raises the money and develops the script. The Executive Producer/UPM or the Cinematographer/Director in many instances is also the Writer.

• PREPRODUCTION: Congratulations, you've got your money, so now the Executive Producer starts to metamorphose into the UPM, looking for cheap, or better yet, free locations, and an individual to actually take responsibility for doing the physical work, a.k.a. a Grip/Gaffer/PA. Meanwhile the Cinematographer/Director gets involved in casting.

• PRODUCTION: Once you're rolling, the Executive Producer/UPM assumes the Script Supervisor's position, while the Cinematographer/Director arranges actors, and, along with the Grip/Gaffer/PA/Sound Man, sets the lights, and then finally shoots the scenes. Someone's spouse or significant other usually gets to be make-up/wardrobe/craft service. Don't forget the Twizzlers.

• POSTPRODUCTION: The Cinematographer/Director now becomes the Editor because he or she is the only one who has been able to follow the erratic sequences thus far. The Executive Producer/UPM/Script Supervisor becomes the Script Supervisor/Assistant Editor and helps keep track of where the various shots and elements are. The Grip/Gaffer/PA becomes a PA/Producer/WebMaster and develops potential distribution channels, while fending off actors and vendors looking for their money.

• DISTRIBUTION: Hopefully the PA/Producer/WebMaster has generated some significant interest and lined up some really good festivals as the three of you head off into the sunset with your hard-earned show and a half-empty canister of Twizzlers.

Cast 'n' crew are the true equity of any production. They are what give the final show its flavor and ambiance. I can basically tell from tenth row center if the people working on a picture were having a good time or not. Don't believe me? Go out and rent *Jurassic Park.* Yeah, I know you've seen it a bunch of times already. But this time look for the magic that made it great. Sure wasn't the story or the dynamic character portrayals. It was the energy; the sheer exuberance of its cast and crew, working in a nurturing environment that gave it the dynamic appeal that made it a blockbuster.

Now go rent something like *Sunset Grill,* made in the dankest of environments by an awkward above-the-line staff. The original script wasn't really all that bad, but "creative" decisions from above the line created an abomination to the craft of cinema. Budget has nothing to do with it. Look at *Water World.* Now there was a lesson waiting to be learned. Yet, sure enough, a little while later comes *The Postman.*

Above-the-line staff today is a wasteland run by ethnic clubs and good ol' boys. Their aging decrepitude is matched only by lack of experience in the young generation of lawyers and MBAs slithering their way into the rotting carapace of the once-great studios.

So far, the independents really haven't stepped up to the plate. Yeah, people like John Cassavetes and John Sayles really gave the indie its start, but that was back in a different age and there were entirely different motivations involved. Were these folks, and more importantly are you, into the independent film because of a passion to work within its unrestricted potential, or merely as a springboard to get a lucrative studio deal?

So far, from what I've seen, the aggregate of the "new generation" of independent films is little more than poorly produced, self-indulgent drivel. Con some marquee-name actor into prancing around in retro fashions and give 'em a gun to wave and retro dialogue to spew, damn, you got a hit on your hands. 'Course, there was *Fargo, Shine,* and a couple of others, but they're the mutated definition of indie. Miramax is widely considered to be the king of the indies but it's really owned by Disney. In fact, most of the avant-garde indie distributors are now owned by big studios.

How ironic that Sundance has turned into the ultimate entrée into Hollywood. At a recent festival I was "hanging" with a notable industry reporter who asked all the filmmakers she came across what they hoped to gain out of their showing there. One hundred percent of them said that they were looking for big Hollywood connections. I'm not whining but rather trying to show you the enormous potential that awaits anyone who can keep enough inherent resolution in their digital media to generate a 35mm projection print with good color saturation.

If only one person reading this book gets it, you could turn this industry around. Now's the time too. Even if you're not into the festival scene, new distribution modalities are coming online as fresh production metaphors emerge every day.

Yes, I know Hollywood's trying to bust into the Internet, but it's a pathetic attempt to get involved in something they don't have a clue about. They actually think that their ability to provide us with an endless supply of "lowest common denominator" content entitles them to some sort of automatic entrance into the world of instantaneous, interpersonal communications.

The new breed of Independents is hopefully going to show us how to tell a good story. 'Course, I could be all wrong. Time will tell.

LIGHT BEAMS & PIXEL STREAMS

Whether your movie is destined for celluloid projection on the big screen or pixel streams on the computer screen, there are common sets of production methodologies that prevail. Once you've got a handle on the basics, all that is left is craft.

We've all been to a store where numerous video cameras are hooked up to video monitors. Many people make qualitative judgments based on this information and are disappointed when the final image quality falls well short. The images of a four-hundred-dollar consumer video camera could well look comparable to a forty-thousand-dollar DigiBeta under these test conditions. All that you're really seeing is the output from the CCD, pumped through a composite encoder and projected on a poorly adjusted, low-end consumer monitor.

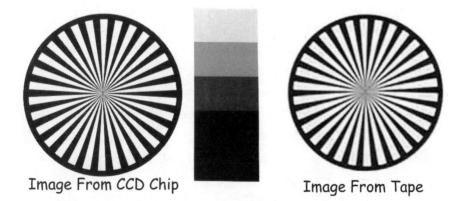

Image From CCD Chip   Image From Tape

The higher the resolution of the recording format, the closer the taped image resembles the image off of the chip, but unless you're recording uncompressed, 4:4:4 RGB, there will always be a noticeable difference. See also the Color Plate on page 195.

The only way to truly evaluate the signals of different cameras and formats is off the tape. Shoot a natural scene under natural light and then shoot a scene under artificial lights. Make sure to include a person, some plants, some brightly colored plastic items and the test chart pages of this book for both color, luminance and resolving power. If you've got a high-quality color printer, you can download some charts from (www.PixelMonger.com) and print them out. Buy yourself a blank videotape, or several if you're comparing formats; set up your charts (see charts on pages 196, 198 and 199 in the Color Plate Section) and shoot them with everything they've got.

Once you've got your tapes, find someone with a vector scope and a wave form monitor, and beg to use the equipment to check your tapes. It is probably safe to say that you should never take any advice regarding signal quality from anyone who doesn't own or use a vector scope and wave form monitors on a regular basis.

The decision of which format to use to shoot your movie and what methodology to use to produce it are far too important to leave to the vagaries of opinion. Learn to think for yourself. Gather your own data from reliable sources who aren't trying to sell you something or looking for company in their own misery. One of the saddest aspects of this industry occurs when some people make a bad decision, or worse yet a series of them; they'll tout their shortcomings as if they were state-of-the-art. Misery loves company and there are an awful lot of miserable people out there who would absolutely love your company.

Once you have the field narrowed down, take the time to digitize a few frames from your final contenders and see how they handle as they pass through your edit environment. Some video compression schemes are more compatible with various edit environments than others.

SIZE DOES MATTER

All things being equal, real estate is one of the major factors in video image quality. The more area that a frame of information consumes, the more inherent resolution is able to be recorded. There are two ways to get a lot of real estate, size and speed, although real estate alone does not guarantee a good image.

All analog and most digital videotape formats record their data in a series of diagonal stripes. These helical scans are placed on the tape by one or more record heads mounted on the outer rim of a spinning drum. Both the drum and the tape are at opposing angles so that the path of the record head writes a track of information diagonally across the tape. The faster the drum moves, the tighter the tracks can be stacked. The faster the tape moves, the more real estate can be covered.

After the tape passes by the rotating drumhead it generally passes a set of fixed heads that write the audio tracks as well as time code and control information.

Originating in the mid '60s, and using a terribly inefficient analog, color-under system, the 3/4" U-matic format is in wider daily operation around the world than any other format. Even now, as we stand firmly rooted in the twenty-first century, the 3/4" U-matic is so ubiquitous that you'd be hard-pressed to find a postproduction house, studio or ad agency that doesn't have one in daily use. In many countries of the world it is still the broadcast standard.

The 3/4" tape appears to have far more real estate, yet the image from the DVCPRO is far superior — while taking up less room. Both formats use a helical scan drum to read and write the video

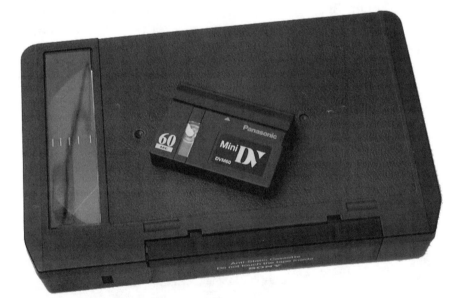

Digital technology is the great equalizer. The tiny DVCPRO tape's format drastically outperforms the much larger cassette's 3/4" U-Matic.

signal to and from the videotape, but it is the speed of the tape through the system and the higher rpm's of the drum that give the DVCPRO the greater resolution.

While the U-matic system moves the 3/4" tape through the system with a drum speed of 3,600 rpm, the DVCPRO moves its 6.3mm tape through at 33.813mm per second with an amazing drum speed of 9,000 rpm. The DVCPRO further optimizes the scheme with which it writes the image stripes on the tape giving it an extremely high real estate value when compared to the U-matic.

The biggest difference between these two formats, perhaps even more important than the resolution issue, is the fact that U-matic is analog composite and DVCPRO is component digital. Each successive copy of an analog format gains contrast and loses resolution, while the DVCPRO can theoretically be cloned thousands of times without degradation. Notice I said "theoretically."

THE SOFT EXPLANATION OF DIGITAL

Perhaps the best way to explain digital is to first compare it to analog. Life itself is analog. From the moment we're born to the day we die, every move we make, every sound we hear, every sight we see is processed in analog. From the ebb and flow of the relentless tides to the very cycle of life that frames our existence, we are analog creatures.

Vision is based on infinitely smooth gradations of tone, from pitch black to blinding white, while color spans the spectrum from infrared to ultraviolet in billions of frequency values. The infinite oscillations and amplitudes of air pressure that transmit sound are a smooth succession of accelerations and decelerations infinitely divisible into smaller and smaller units of mass/energy. Analog is analogous to infinite.

Digital, on the other hand, is quite finite. Digital is the representation of analog in binary quanta. Any physical event that can be seen or heard can also be reduced to numbers. The more numbers you use to describe something, the closer to the analog form it comes, but it can never describe the analog event exactly. There is of course Blumenfeld's Theorem '86 which states, "Given enough bits/resolution you could sample down to the molecular level and restate reality in the digital domain."

I am particularly fond of the Dutch Masters, and can easily stand for hours in front of a Pieter Claesz while the flow of humanity silently washes around me. Using a simple search engine you can pull up one of his surreal masterpieces. It will, of course be a digital representation of the original and as such is limited to the color palette and tonal limitations of your particular computer system. Is it a good indicator of the original? Yes, but no matter how high the resolution of a digital recording gets, it will never be able to capture the true depth of color and texture that are present in the original analog painting.

All digital recording technology comes down to creating a "good enough" approximation, and what is good enough for viewing on your home television is quite simply *not* good enough to print to film and project on a large screen.

THE HARD EXPLANATION OF DIGITAL

Digital is an electronic method of expressing an analog event in numeric equivalent. Visual elements within the digital domain are translated into a cluster of PIXELS or PIcture ELements. Contrary to popular belief, a PIXEL is not a resolute or finite amount of data, but rather a potential of resolution. It is not a 1:1 map-out.

By using recording devices that can translate sound or light waves into voltage, and then sampling those voltages, we can arrive at numeric equivalents for the analog values. This is called analog-to-digital (A/D) conversion.

These values are then expressed in a binary code which is composed of ones and zeros (actually electrical impulses in a mostly "on" state or a mostly "off" state). Binary is the language of computers. It is a language of just two words, yes and no. It isn't so much that computers have found their way into the entertainment industry, as film and video have found their way into the computer's realm. Anything that uses a two-word language is essentially a computer peripheral.

Each digit in this binary code is a bit (Binary digIT). Each mathematical bit can define one of two states, on or off, black or white, yes or no, 0 or 1. Two bits can define four levels, three bits eight, four bits sixteen, and so on, using the simple formula 2n, where n equals the number of bits. To imagine just how much information can be expressed in binary terms, consider human DNA, which is a 4-bit code (A-C-G-T).

Eight bits together make a byte, which can describe 256 levels of brightness or color. A signal that is converted into a ten-bit number can describe over 5,000 levels of brightness or color; and sixteen bits more than 65,000. Obviously, all things being equal, a 10-bit system will generate better-looking images.

Unlike the base-10 decimal system we all grew up with ("dec" meaning 10), the binary system of digital computing is base 2. Since it can only describe two states (on/off) it requires a far greater number of digits to express a value. The base 10 number 230 is expressed in binary form as

43

11100110. The result of a binary multiplication contains the sum of digits of the original numbers so: 1100100 X 11100110 = 101100111011000 (in base 10, 175 X 212 = 37,100).

This preponderance of digits that the binary system generates is where the initial opportunity for compression becomes most evident. Given too low a bit depth, large areas with subtle variations in color have a tendency to create distinct bands.

COMPRESSION SCHEMES

Compression is a difficult topic to describe, because the results are so subjective. With television and desktop video, the general gauge

Compression artifacts become more evident with greater compression. The image here was compressed at 50:1.

is the eye of the beholder. Does it look good or not? Once we get into the realm of video-for-film, however, the subjective critique becomes far less relevant, and we need to look at mathematical justification for platform and methodological decisions.

Talk to any relatively knowledgeable video engineer and you're going to spend a lot of time on the topic of compression schemes. They are, after all, what make nearly everything digital possible. We're still years away from being able to record, broadcast or store the enormous amounts of data that we deal with every day without these sophisticated algorithms. The important word in "compression scheme" is scheme. The dictionary defines a scheme as:

1) NOUN: a method devised for making or doing something or attaining an end.
Synonyms: plan, blueprint, design, game plan, project, strategy.
Related: conception, idea, notion, ground plan, intention, platform, purpose, means, method, way.

2) NOUN: a secret plan for accomplishing a usually evil or unlawful end.
Synonyms: plot, cabal, conspiracy, coven, intrigue, machination, practice.
Related: collusion, complicity, contraption, contrivance, artifice, maneuver, ruse, stratagem, trick.

Now, it would be nice to think that the first definition is the one we're dealing with, but I'm afraid not. Compression is a war fought by really big corporations, and the winner makes all the bucks. Compression engineers spend nearly every waking hour trying to figure out how to get a video signal to *look* good without really *being* good. The first rule of compression is to remove everything from the signal that you possibly can.

From birth the human eye is tuned to subtle shifts in the gray scale. It is these subtle shifts of light and shadow that transmit the play of emotion across the human face. We are so subliminally sensitive to these subtle shifts that our eyes can detect a mere 0.1% shift in luminosity. Fortunate for the compression mongers, we're simply not as sensitive to the color spectrum, so this is where they focus their efforts.

Since the human eye is most sensitive to green, the red and blue elements of the video signal are sampled at half the rate. The unfortunate result of this scheme is that it deeply affects the quality of skin tone. Even in the very best video environments, skin tones lack the depth and subtlety that we find in film images. This, perhaps more than any other factor, is why so many digital film projects end up in black and white.

If you understand the basics of compression and how it affects the color-space of your image, you will be able to create a production environment that not only meets your financial limitations, but also maintains what little color information is left in today's highly compressed digital video formats.

THE MANY FLAVORS OF COMPRESSION

There is absolutely no way to fully explain the convoluted world of compression without filling many pages with multi-syllabic words. Basically, higher compression factors allow data to flow faster, while lower compression ratios give a better picture.

Anyone who's worked with PhotoShop or one of the other personal computer graphics packages is already familiar with the basics of compression as it pertains to a single image. JPEG is quite rightly the most popular flavor of single-image compression and stands for the Joint Photographic Experts Group, ISO/ITU-T, while MPEG stands for Moving Picture Experts Group, ISO/CCITT.

JPEG baseline compression essentially transforms images into 8 x 8 pixel blocks of frequency and amplitude data. Since digital data is essentially written in ones and zeros, this scheme looks more closely at the less visible high frequencies, and compresses them by a higher factor than it does the more visible lower frequencies. Many normally dense data blocks can subsequently be reduced to a single one or zero.

MPEG adds inter-frame compression to the basic JPEG scheme, essentially looking for similarities between frames and averaging common elements. There are several flavors of MPEG, the most common being MPEG-2, which is the backbone for HDTV, DVD and digital TV. MPEG-2, with data rates between 4 and 100 Mb/s, is essentially designed to be a transmission strategy utilizing decoders at the reception end of the data stream.

MPEG-2's method of using inter-frame compression to remove redundancy within sequential frames creates long *groups of pictures* (GOPs). This method of producing strings of pictures containing I (header), P (predictive) and B (bi-directional) frames, makes it quite undesirable as a digital film production tool.

THE ITU AND YOU

With the myriad formats and compression schemes out there, some-one had to step in and start dealing with standardization issues. The CCIR (Comité Consultatif International des Radiocommunications) was widely considered the last word in transmission standards; but the unmistakable French twist that was put on everything became tiring, and broadcasters and manufacturers the world over looked to the United Nations for some relief.

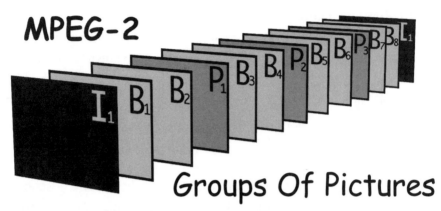

MPEG-2

Groups Of Pictures

Although an efficient method of compression, the sequential GOPs cause difficulty when trying to create frame-accurate edit points.

The UN came through and formed the International Telecommunications Union (ITU) as a regulatory body covering all forms of broadcast communication. The CCIR was absorbed into the ITU after a judicious amount of whining from ze French, and the rest, as they say, is history. We now have an internationally recognized body of egghead engineers that sets standards that everyone follows.

The reason I bring up the ITU at all is that without a point of reference, there is really no place to start.

601 VIDEO, NOT 601 JEANS

The granddaddy of all video standards is unquestionably ITU-R-601, formerly known as CCIR-601. This international standard for digitizing component video in both 525 and 625 line systems is the basis for numerous video formats, including D1 (uncompressed) and Digital BetaCam (compressed). It deals with both the RGB video signal that comes directly off of the imaging chips in cameras and image generators like computers, as well as color difference systems like (Y, R-Y, B-Y). If you've got access to a personal computer with a high-quality video digitizer board you'll most likely find connectors for one or both systems on the system's break-out box.

Every relevant form of digital recording has its own compression schemes. ITU-R 601 accommodates the highest practical compression standard for modest budgeted video-to-film purposes. Essentially the 601 standard breaks the visual spectrum down into three units using either an 8-bit or 10-bit system. As the electronic signal comes off the three CCDs of a professional quality video camera, they are described in ITU-R 601 lingo as a RGB 4:4:4. The first four describe the luminance value of the picture; the second two describe the color.

The business end of the highly popular Media100.

If you were to up-convert that image and print it directly to film, you would be amazed at the quality of the projected image. It would possess tonal gradation and color saturation that would rival the projected image of a fast 35mm stock.

On the flip side, if you take the same image, sample it at a high compression ratio, record it to a low bandwidth recording medium, then de-compress it and re-compress it through several different schemes, and then print it to the same film stock — you will understand why the vast majority of video-to-film projects end up looking the way they do.

I've been up-converting and printing the 601 signal to film for more than a decade now, and every year, better and better algorithms and processes show up to further facilitate the process. The first 601 up-conversion algorithm I used was written by Price Pethal, a true luminary in the digital film industry and co-founder of Jim Cameron's Digital Domain.

Pethal's code allowed me to create more than sixty-five visual effects for Roger Corman's *Fantastic Four* in ITU-R 601 and then up-convert and print to film. Unfortunately for our micro-budgeted movie, Twentieth Century-Fox bought out the rights after just one screening. They figured that if we could do that much with no budget then they could do something really great with the budget of a small country. And there it sits.

I've used 601 up-conversion more than a hundred times since that 1990 project, in movies with both large and small budgets. The substantial amount of up-conversion algorithms and printer drivers that now deal with the ITU-R 601 protocol have made it the most widely accepted video-to-film format in the industry. HiDef is coming on strong and I now use it quite often, but it is still too volatile a production environment to use for your first few projects.

ITU-R 601 makes an irrefutable, qualitative and quantitative standard by which all other platforms can be judged and evaluated. Once you understand the technical aspects of 601 you'll be able to make solid judgments regarding your own production platform choices. Without a qualitative reference to base your decisions on, you're only guessing — or worse yet, following someone else's advice.

• *While RGB theoretically creates the most robust ITU-R 601 signal, the most common reference to 601 is as color difference, component digital video, sampled at 4:2:2 at 13.5 MHz with 720 luminance samples per active line, digitized at either 8 or 10 bits.* Whew, it hurt to write it too.

We're going to spend the remainder of this chapter deciphering that last sentence because once you understand 601 you'll have enough information to begin making educated decisions... and hopefully you'll never have to turn your work of art into a retro-artsy-fartsy, black-and-white motion picture... unless you really want to.

• *The ITU-R 601 signal can have either an RGB or color difference format.*

As light enters the camera's lens it is focused on by a light-sensitive computer chip called a Charge Coupled Device (CCD). The surface of the CCD is composed of thousands, if not millions, of microscopic cells that act as tiny light meters, each generating an electrical charge proportional to the light striking it. The relative current from each element is then sent to an encoder where it is converted from the analog RGB, 4:4:4 video to digital component and streamed down a wire where it is inserted as binary information into the steady flow of ones and zeros that represent the data structure of the recording environment.

Most of the video acquisition formats that digital filmmakers use convert the RGB signal into a (Y, B-Y, R-Y) component video signal. Although not 100% accurate, without going into several pages of really boring technical palaver, think of (Y) as representing the analog luminance or inherent light range of the image, while (R-Y) and (B-Y) represent the two color difference signals. (R-Y) is RED MINUS LUMINANCE and (B-Y) is BLUE MINUS LUMINANCE. Since Y encompasses R, G and B, a simple math equation (R-Y + B-Y = G) will yield G.

• *ITU-R 601 signal is component digital video.*

There are several methods of maintaining the initial integrity of the video signal by keeping various elements of the signal (components) separate. The most common way of doing this is by simply using individual wires for each signal component.

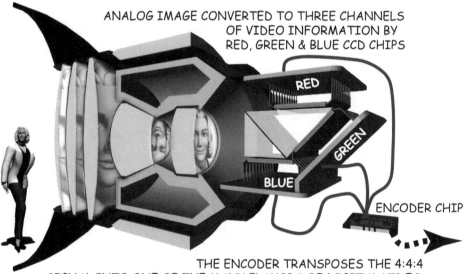

ANALOG IMAGE CONVERTED TO THREE CHANNELS
OF VIDEO INFORMATION BY
RED, GREEN & BLUE CCD CHIPS

RED

GREEN

BLUE

ENCODER CHIP

THE ENCODER TRANSPOSES THE 4:4:4
SIGNAL INTO ONE OF THE MANY FLAVORS OF DIGITAL VIDEO

RGB is the most robust signal type due to the purity and wider palette of its colors. The Red, Green, Blue and sync (timing) signals are carried on separate wires. Most computer systems are based on an RGB color system. For studio work I often attach an RGB break-out box directly to my three-chip camera and feed the uncompressed RGB component signal directly into a Targa videographic board which digitizes, compresses and lays the video directly to disk. This method maintains a high level of color integrity and works extremely well for effects shots.

Component Video separates each of the three colors and luminance by one of several methods and is used in BetacamSP, DigitalBetacam, D1, DVCPRO and other high quality formats. A component signal is generally expressed as YUV but you'll also see it written as (Y, R-Y, B-Y) or (YCrCb). Component video signals, such as ITU-R 601 retain maximum luminance and chrominance bandwidth for a much longer time. They are far more robust within an edit and graphic environment; and if you ever need to pull a chroma key or do any sort of luminance mapping, you're definitely going to want the extra color-space that component signals provide.

This break-out accessory attaches to the back of the camcorder's imaging unit and allows the signal to be pulled directly from the CCD chips.

S-Video is often considered a component signal. Technically it does keep the color and luminance routed through two separate wires, but the inherent quality of the signal is so low that it is unfit for consideration as a digital production format. Unfortunately S-Video systems like Hi8 are quite popular due to their low cost, and while they are generally far better than using a standard composite video format, they fall far short of a true component system signal.

Composite Video merges the R, G, B, luminance and sync information into a single wire. The lower-quality image is intended for "end use" and does not make a viable production environment. The television broadcast standard for the United States, in fact anywhere in

Containing the widest variety of flavors in the industry, the Targa3000 break-out box is a hot item for desktop moviemakers.

the world that runs on 60Hz electrical power, is NTSC (National Television Systems Committee, also known as Never The Same Color). NTSC specifies a composite signal with a total of 525 vertical scan lines, 40 of which are used for vertical blanking. This leaves a visible image area 480 lines high.

• ITU-R 601 signal is sampled at 4:2:2 at 13.5 Mhz.

At this time, 4:4:4 is the highest practical ratio of sampling frequencies used to digitize the luminance and color difference

BNC, S-video and RCA are all various types of video connectors. Generally, if you see BNC connectors, you're dealing with a professional system, while the Apple ADB cable makes a great S-video connector.

components of a video signal. All arguments and discussions about which video format prints to film best end here, because uncompressed, 10-bit, 4:4:4 is essentially the Holy Grail of digital filmmakers. In the 4:4:4 signal there are equal numbers of samples of all components. (Y) gets 4 samples, (R-Y) gets 4 samples, and (B-Y) gets 4 samples = 4:4:4.

There is of course 4:4:4:4, which denotes the addition of an Alpha channel, as well as various uber-resolutions such as 8:4:4 and 27 Mhz:13.5:13.5; but for the foreseeable future, 4:4:4 is going to do just fine.

Since most television and video systems operate on lower-quality ratios like 4:1:1 or 4:2:0 we generally never get to see 4:4:4 resolution video in our daily life. Most quality personal computers use a native 8-bit, RGB 4:4:4 system but the signal is generally downsampled by video I/O boards to a far less robust resolution. When 4:4:4 images are generated within a computer and then taken directly from the computer's hard drive as data files, up-converted, and printed to film, the resultant images compare well to images originating on film.

It would be really great if ITU-R 601 maintained the color information that came off the chips and sampled at full 4:4:4, but it doesn't. ITU-R 601 is generally considered a 4:2:2 system where the color is sampled at half the rate as the luminance information. The 4 represents a sampling frequency of 13.5 MHz, while each of the 2s represent a sample frequency of 6.75 MHz. Thus 4:2:2 has half the color information of the more robust 4:4:4.

Most DV cameras transpose their signal into a 4:1:1 configuration, which essentially has 256 levels of sampling, compared with the 1,024 levels at 4:2:2.

• *ITU-R 601 generates 720 luminance samples per active line.*

In analog monitors a scan line is called a raster (to be technically accurate a raster is actually the entire screen) and a frame is made up of two sets of them. The cathode ray sweeps across the screen and after completing one horizontal scan line the beam shuts off (horizontal blanking) and returns to start each line after the next.

In an interlaced system (like television) every odd-numbered raster (line) is written as a field and then the beam goes back to the top and writes the even-numbered rasters. These two fields create an interlaced frame. In NTSC there are thirty of them (really 29.97) per second, offset by color burst.

In a progressive scan environment (similar to a computer monitor) each line is written in succession until the beam hits the bottom and snaps back up to the top.

ODD + EVEN = INTERLACED FRAME

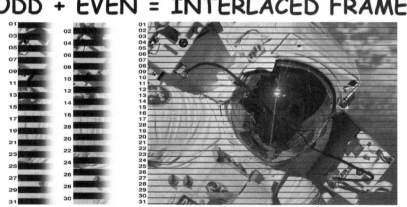

It takes two sets of interlaced rasters to build a solid frame of video.

In LCD and plasma monitors the fields are always on rather than being traced one at a time. This is why you don't need any special accommodations to film or videotape them. In NTSC digital systems the visible image area is 480 pixels high and 720 pixels wide. *Pixel is the abbreviation of Picture Element, which is the binary representation of a sample of luminance and chrominance.*

The ITU-R 601 digital signal generates a separate and distinct luminance sample for 345,600 pixels, thirty times a second.

• *The ITU-R 601 signal is digitized at either 8 or 10 bits.*

Progressive scan builds the image using a continuous succession of rasters.

ITU-R 601 allows for both the luminance and chrominance information (pixels) to be sampled at either 8 bits or 10 bits. The vast majority of televisions, as well as PC computers, Macintosh included, are 8-bit. This means that each component in the (Y, B-Y, R-Y) signal is represented by 256 levels of information. A 10-bit system creates a palette that has more than 5,000 levels of information. Since you stand a good chance of losing information every time you move or manipulate your information, it is in your best interest to give serious consideration to using a format with the greatest bit depth you can afford.

Many times motion picture effects work is specified in 10-bit log and generally needs to be done on a 10-bit system like Silicon

Graphics. Recently software applications such as Puffin Designs Commotion have appeared on the PC and Mac platforms, allowing 10-bit work to be done in an 8-bit world.

One of the standard production metaphors for visual effects work is to scan film into data files using a 10-bit, SGI/RGB file format at full sample (4:4:4). As long as the RGB image format is compatible with the software systems used, there will be no further degradation of the image. When the image is printed back to film using the same I/O system the resulting frames should closely match the originals.

In the motion picture *Barb Wire*, we had far more shots to do than our meager budget would allow. Rather than scan each frame individually we took the numerous shots that originated on 35mm film stock and telecined them to 4:2:2 RGB image files. Unlike scanning where an electron beam painstakingly records each individual frame three times (R+G+B), telecini runs the film through in real time, turning each frame of film into an ITU-R 601 image file. The resultant data file is much smaller than a scanned file and far less expensive. (Note: For what it's worth, the first day of shooting on the movie was done with my mini-DV camcorder.)

If you figure around a megabyte per frame with an average effects sequence running five or six seconds, plus head and tails chime in at several hundred megabytes a shot — ten years ago that was a lot of storage. Nowadays, you can slip it into a shirt pocket and have room left over for a phone and a palmtop computer.

After adding effects in various software applications (Commotion, After Effects, Electric Image) the images were up-converted and sent to the printer as 4:2:2 RGB data files, printed to film and edited into the motion picture. Many of the effects shots were cut in amongst the non-affected shots without any noticeable resolution difference.

WHERE DID ALL MY COLOR GO?

DV, the format of choice for a vast majority of digital film-makers, uses a native compression scheme of 5:1 from a 4:1:1 bit-sampled source. The luminance channel receives four samples at 13.5 MHz while the two color channels receive only single samples of 3.75 MHz each. The relatively high compression scheme (5:1) of DVCPRO strips much of the color information from the otherwise robust signal. When combined with the low sample rate (4:1:1), you end up with a signal that looks great when played back on your monitor, but performs quite poorly in chrominance values when up-converted and printed to film.

In a 4:4:4 sampled signal, 66% of the information deals with color. In a 4:1:1 sampled signal with 5:1 compression, only 16% of the signal deals with color. After just a few seemingly harmless conversions and transpositions, the delicate signal often ends up with only 5% or 6% of its original color.

By shooting your movie on video you stand to save enormously when compared to the inherent costs of film-based production. The trade-offs are the wide-ranging advantages inherent in film itself; the look, the texture, the resolution and subtlety. While this book will endeavor to get you as close as possible to the classic cinematic film look, it should be obvious that there is absolutely no way to fully emulate the richness of film. We are locked into a battle of perception, and every wrong step you make will take you further away from a film-like image.

FORMAT WARS

There has been a fierce, global battle raging for the latter half of this century. The battlefield is littered with dead or dying formats, and you have just parachuted into hostile territory. Your survival depends on developing a set of strategic objectives and avoiding the land mines of propaganda.

Technology before the chip didn't move all that fast. Yeah, there were innovations, but real breakthroughs were few and far between. Back when countries were trying to figure out what television standard they were going to use, there was a lot of confusion. Competing formats, some good, some not so good, all backed by companies touting the particular benefits of their particular electromechanical hodgepodge.

NTSC vs. PAL

Bottom line is that everyone was basically selling the same thing with a regional twist. In the end, countries that had an electrical infrastructure based on 60 Hz like the U.S., Japan, Canada and Central America went with the 30 frames per second (60 fields) of NTSC. Countries with a 50 Hz infrastructure like most of Europe, Great Britain, Australia and China went with the 25 frames per second (50 fields) format of PAL. Then of course there were the French who, as a point of national pride, had to do something totally contrary, so they came up with SECAM.

Iraq and Iran didn't want France to feel alone so they adopted SECAM as well. Except for the holy trinity of retro-tech, what we essentially ended up with was a world split by two formats, NTSC (National Television Standards Committee) and PAL (Phase Alternating Line).

THE DAYS BEFORE TAPE

Now keep in mind that when these standards were first introduced, there wasn't any videotape yet. All the early television shows were shot live and broadcast directly to the home. If you wanted to record a show for posterity you simply filmed the television screen with a motion picture camera (kinescope). If you wanted to re-broadcast a kinescoped show you simply projected it on a wall and aimed a video camera at it.

One of the reasons that there are so few old shows and movies around is because the motion picture film back then was still constructed from Thomas Edison's original cellulose nitrate formula (we now use cellulose acetate). In addition to being fragile and sensitive to humidity, the stuff was combustible — explosive really — and many old shows and movies soon went the way of an errant match or cigarette butt.

THE TECHNOLOGY OF RUST

Years later (1955), after experimenting with all kinds of recording media (metallic wire was one of my favorites), AMPEX came up with the "rust scrapings on scotch tape" concept, and the era of videotape had begun.

SCOTTY'S HOME SCIENCE PROJECT

Take a piece of rusty metal and sandpaper off the metal oxide (rust) until you've got yourself a nice little pile. Then take a roll of Scotch Tape® and stretch out a good yard or so with the glue side facing up. Sprinkle your rust dust over the tape until the whole thing is covered and work it in really well with a soup spoon.

Let the whole thing sit for an hour or two and then brush off the excess oxide with a paintbrush. Take a soft cloth (T-shirts work well), and buff up the side with the rust on it. If you run this tape across the heads of a tape recorder while in record mode and then run the same tape across the head at relatively the same speed in play mode you'll hear an amazingly good rendition of what you just recorded. (Note: It's a good idea to have a bottle of isopropyl alcohol and a cotton swab on hand to clean up the mess.)

Mid-century analog technology wasn't based on exotic materials or micro-miniature componentry. You took a little of this, and hooked it to a little one of these, put on a couple 'o lights and a nice set of dials and voilà! A new, improved thing. Still firmly rooted in the last fading vestiges of the mechanical age, engineers all used the same raw materials to create the various video production environments.

Back in those technologically slower days, data flowed pretty much at the same speed for everyone. Well, except the French. Processors, whether NTSC or PAL, still pushed their analog data signal through copper wires at relatively the same speed. Since NTSC was pushing more frames per second through the same copper wire (30 as opposed to 25), it reduced the signal bandpass (the amount of data each frame carried) accordingly.

There are really so many valid arguments for using PAL over NTSC that I could fill an entire book with them. Instead, I have assembled my favorite arguments and offer them here, greatly abbreviated, for your consideration.

DROP-FRAME

NTSC generates 525 visible lines of image at 60 fields per second, or 525/60. Remember that two fields make a frame. When color was introduced to the NTSC system the frame rate was changed from an even 30 frames per second to the current 29.97 fps (Drop-Frame). Two frames were dropped every minute to compensate for a timing metaphor used in commercial programming. It was nothing so technically involved that your basic chimpanzee couldn't figure it out and accommodate, but back then they figured that reducing time by .1% would make things easier for people even dumber than simians — network schedulers.

Drop-Frame is only one of the many reasons that I'm not a big fan of using NTSC for film applications. Many cameras can operate in DF (Drop Frame) or ND (Non-Drop), and while there is no effect on the actual frame rate, there are problems everywhere along the production process. Not only does this complicate everything from synchronizing peripheral production equipment to computing edit points, it also brings a nice hairy fly into the ointment of video-to-film transposition as well.

Frame Rate

PAL generates 625 lines of visible lines of image at 50 fields per second or 625/50, while NTSC uses a frame rate of 29.97, or

525/60. NTSC has a wonkey frame rate of 29.97, while PAL uses a very solid 25 fps timing.

When you process your NTSC video for up-conversion to film's 24 frames per second, you first need to drop six frames out of the thirty (a whopping 20% reduction) in total information right from the start.

• *The PAL frame rate is 20% more efficient than NTSC for Video to Film.*

Since film generates 24 frames per second, anyone with an above-room temperature IQ will see the obvious benefits in establishing a video production environment based on 25 fps as opposed to 30 fps, when producing for a 24 fps end-product. I've been using PAL for motion picture applications for many years and in all that time I've never had anyone mention or notice the extra frame.

I'm often asked about synchronizing sound between the 24 and 25 fps frame rates. To start with, there is no such thing as perfect sync. Not in film, not in video, not in life. The farther away you are physically from another person, the further out of sync that person is. Any form of locking the audio to a picture entails a bit of work and artistry. I prefer to do that work on a signal that is significantly superior.

Vanilla Video

There are so many flavors of resolution, and so many ways it can be stated that you can almost feel your leg being tugged every time someone mentions the word. Since resolution is affected initially by the camera's lens (a topic I'm quite fond of ranting on about), as well as by numerous other factors in the image stream, let's first talk about inherent resolution, the theoretical, all-things-being-equal type of resolution that the system is supposed to have.

Lines of Image

Essentially, resolution is a measure of the detail that can be resolved, or reproduced in the image. The ITU-R 601 digital video standard defines the NTSC, 525/60 signal as having 486 active vertical lines, each with 720 horizontal samples. ITU-R 601 defines the PAL, 625/50 signal as having 576 active vertical lines, each having 720 horizontal samples. There are 51 more vertical lines of image in the PAL system than in NTSC. (See page 193 in the Color Plate Section)

• *PAL has 11% more vertical resolution than NTSC for Video to Film.*

Sample Rate

The transposition of the analog image voltage off the camera's CCD chips into a series of digital values is called sampling. The more samples there are per second, the higher the number of bits into which the image data can be resolved. PAL is sampled at 17.7 MHz while NTSC is sampled at 14.3 MHz. The ITU-R 601 standard defines a full sample rate (4) as 13.5.

• *PAL has a 14% higher sampled resolution than NTSC for Video to Film.*

Both NTSC-D1 and PAL-D1 use non-square pixels. While this generally doesn't cause any problem as long as you maintain a native format data path, the moment you divert the signal into a non-native environment, like say, a computer program, you're going to need to deal with the variations in pixel aspect ratio.

NTSC-D1 uses a 0.9 pixel aspect ratio that is 0.9 wide and 1.0 high, orientated in the vertical direction. PAL-D1 on the other hand, uses a pixel aspect ratio of 1.0666 that is oriented horizontally. Since PAL's vertical resolution is noticeably greater than that of NTSC, the increased horizontalization of the pixel's aspect gives more potential "wide-screen" resolution.

Aspect ratio issues aside, PAL is by far the simplest format to work with, even in the United States. Computers just don't care and easily adapt to various pixel aspect ratios. Nonlinear edit systems don't care, and the vast majority of professional monitors have a simple switch on the faceplate to switch from NTSC to PAL.

So am I advocating the use of PAL over NTSC? Depends. For me it is as simple to work with as NTSC, with big payoffs in resolution. But then I've been doing this digital-to-film thing for quite a while. I've also got a rather firm grasp of the technologies involved, and my own rather odious production system that has evolved over the years. For someone who has a good practical understanding of the technologies involved, PAL is a no-brainer; but for someone starting out, the best NTSC system you can get your hands on is probably going to serve you well. The important thing to keep in mind is that with NTSC, you're starting out with a significant handicap.

INTERLACED VS. NON-INTERLACED

Interlaced video is laid down in two fields of odd and even lines of image (rasters). Two of these fields equal a frame. Non-interlaced video is laid down in successive lines of image. CRT computer monitors operate this way, so it's one of the reasons that type is much easier to read on a computer monitor that on a television.

There are several cameras that are capable of shooting both interlaced and non-interlaced video. In the consumer range you've got cameras like the Canon Optura, and in the broadcast range you've got the new generation of DVCPRO and High-Definition (HD). While it does require a much higher bandwidth to accommodate the higher data rate, the vertical resolution (represented by the total of its lines) does not exhibit the dithering of detail that is found in interlaced pictures.

Now you'd think that, when you're considering a video format that is eventually going to be printed to film, a good non-interlaced signal would be the obvious choice. It does after all, more closely emulate the film frame by representing a single uniform image, and it also looks absolutely great when displayed on a monitor.

If you're shooting in PAL or better yet, with one of the new 24 fps Hi-Def cameras, progressive scan is often the best way to go. A solid frame of digital information equals a solid frame of film. If, however, you're using an NTSC system, remember that 1/5 of your frames must be thrown away for every second you transpose to film. That's six out of every thirty frames, totally discarded.

In addition to causing many transpositional problems in the up-conversion and printing process, the loss of so many frames creates a flickering image that is inherently distasteful to many audiences.

FRAME FOR FILM

This may sound obvious, but the number of people who are taken by surprise when they finally see their image cropped to the wider aspect of cinema is astounding. If you've shot in standard NTSC 4:3 then you've got to throw away upwards of 20% of your hard-earned image. Talk to any printer and you'll get a wealth of stories about digital filmmakers who lost important information in their scenic composition.

Take your pick of 1.85 or 16 x 9 and stick to it. If your viewfinder doesn't have a cinematic reticule (framing template or outline) then make one. I'm predisposed to the 16 x 9 format because it makes your movie inherently more marketable to cable and network. Since you'll now match the standard Hi-Def broadcast aspect ratio, very little side information is lost in projecting to the more cinematic 1.85.

Keep in mind that most pro-summer cameras don't really generate a true 16 x 9 image, but rather crop upwards of 25% of the signal off the CCDs to get the "wide look." Some other camcorders stretch the conventional 4 x 3 image to the wider aspect ratio. Be sure you're dealing with a true 16 x 9 image system and not throwing away precious resolution before committing to a wide aspect format. D-Beta and most high-end DVCPRO camcorders use a true 16 x 9 CCD to record the image.

Arguments can be made with regard to the commercial broadcast of a movie shot in 4 x 3, but when you look at all the options, weigh all the pluses and minuses back and forth, you'll generally come to the same conclusion. It's far better to maintain all the inherent vertical resolution that you can for as long as you can. Letterbox your movie for network release in 4 x 3 systems. The new world order of 16 x 9 will be around a long, long time. Anything shot or released in 4 x 3 is, quite simply, ancient history.

TOOLS OF THE TRADE

As long as you have freedom of choice, exercise it. And most importantly don't believe any salespeople, advertisements, articles or books (even mine) that offer a quick and painless solution.

The only way to evaluate what is right for you is to poke around and try it yourself. What might be the correct solution for one person could be extreme overkill for another. Whether your budget ranges from the several hundred dollars that a second-hand Hi8 and used Mac would cost you, to an $80,000, fully built G4/DigiBeta system with a Media100xr, the truly important considerations are aptitude and talent — and maybe cash flow.

FORMAT CHOICE

I'm assuming that you've plowed through the Tech section, and now have a profound understanding of what constitutes a robust signal and how important it is to nurture and maintain it. If, like so many creative, right-brained people you've skipped that section entirely, there is a bit of review in this chapter as we analyze the benefits of the various production environments.

The actual decision of which format and computer platform to go with comes down to the Price/Performance ratio. What system quite simply gives you the most bang for the buck?

Choices are rather simple in the motion picture world. The industry's slow growth allowed parallel systems to evolve. The same piece of

35mm film fits into a 1949 Mitchell BNC or a 2000 Panavision Millennium. There are many different camera manufacturers, all catering to different preferences based on what you shoot and where you live. Panavision, Arriflex, Aaton, and Cinema Products took the high ground, with other smaller manufacturers picking up the niche markets of high-speed, ultra-light weight, under-water, stunt, and so on. All in all, it's been a rather mellow, high-quality field of competition.

The world would have shrunk a lot sooner if video manufacturers had gotten together and settled on industry-wide standards. But then I guess, that's why we've got the Web.

With video formats you need to consider signal quality, resolution, color-space and data rates. Computer platform decisions should concern ease of use, software applications, data rates and cost factors. Every aspect of signal quality can be used like a game of Three-Card Monty. What might sound like the best quality based on compression might actually not be the best based on data rates.

Obviously, you want to use the highest resolution you can afford, but there's a whole lot more to resolution than just the number of pixels on your CCD chip. Filmmaking is a process, and the images must overcome a number of hurdles. If you hook the video out from a number of different cameras to identical video monitors, they'll all give you a relatively nice image. What you don't see is what that image looks like once it is recorded. Different formats may suffer due to inferior electronics or poor lenses. The actual speed of the tape has a major effect upon the signal's integrity. The methodology employed to record color and luminance information has a direct bearing on how robust the signal is.

When you finally plunk down your hard-earned cash, every buck you waste on equipment is a buck that doesn't go up on the screen, so...

- GET YOUR HANDS DIRTY: You can delegate the process of gathering information and trying out various systems, but you can't delegate the final decisions. Before you open the checkbook at least one person who's ass is on the line needs to actually learn and understand the technologies and the basic operation of the systems you're going to use. If you rely on a salesperson or someone who isn't invested in the production, then you're too far removed, and a world of pain and disappointment is waiting just around the corner. There is far too much snake oil in this industry to rely on anything but hands-on trial and error.

- BUY GOOD EQUIPMENT FROM A QUALITY VENDOR: Those deals in the back of magazines might look tempting, but where are the vendors when your nifty new camcorder starts eating tapes for breakfast or your hard drive crashes the day before a screening? This stuff is twitchy and if you think you're just going to "plug and play" you are painfully wrong. Service, even for battle-weary old curmudgeons like me, is as important as the technology.

- BEWARE OF BUZZWORDS: Don't allow buzzwords to serve as verbal shortcuts until you've clearly communicated that you understand exactly what they're supposed to mean. Phrases like "enhanced resolution" or "widescreen emulation" may sound great but generally mean that the manufacturer is just trying to keep up with the market without actually improving the merchandise.

- STICK WITH THE SIMPLEST TECHNOLOGY THAT WORKS FOR YOU: The whole thing about computers and digital technology is that it's supposed to make things easier; yet nearly every industry magazine spends page after page comparing tweakie little features between competing products. Did you know that 90% of the people use 10% of the features of any given digital product, whether hardware or software? Let's say you have a choice between two cameras, and they both create identical images. The one with fewer features is probably not only going to save you money, but will probably be far more dependable and much easier to use. You don't want to be on a hot set reading the instruction manual.

- FAVOR "PROVEN" OVER "BREAKTHROUGH": After "doing time" on the bleeding edge of digital production, you'll start to recognize a certain type of person who is always extolling the virtues of the "newest hardware" that's "supposed to be" better than everything else on the market. Don't risk system downtime on something that isn't proven. Time after time, a battle-proven system will get you to the premiere more dependably, and that is what it's all about.

- IF IT AINT BROKE, DON'T FIX IT: Avoid all upgrades once you're in production! The real cost of a major hardware or software upgrade is lost time and productivity. Even though the manufacturer, sales people and every magazine in the industry tells you that the new improved upgrade is ten times better, stick to the flavor that works. There is also the chance that one small, seemingly insignificant change in the linking together of disparate systems (concatenation) can have a compounding effect on the final image quality.

- BUY IN THE "SWEET SPOT": The "sweet spot" is the nego-
  tiable area between too expensive and too old. Don't necessarily
  go for the most expensive or newest gear you can find because
  you're going to end up paying through the nose. Who wants to
  be in the middle of production when their spiffy new camcorder
  is recalled?

From mini-DV to Hi-Def, the choices and costs are endless. Like any
determination regarding major investments, you want to make your
decision based on qualified and quantifiably sound information.

It's really hard to figure this all out on your own. If you live in Los
Angeles, you can always pick up the latest buzz just hanging out at
the local watering hole or one of the many SIGs (Special Interest
Groups) L.A. is famous for. If you, like the majority of digital
moviemakers, live in some godforsaken backwater like, say, San
Francisco, Chicago or New York, well then you're going to need to
buffer your data banks by virtual means.

Several notable industry magazines maintain both an online presence
as well as their more conventional dead-tree editions. *Videography*
Magazine has covered the digital age since it was just a nasty
rumor, and has some of the most respected names in the industry
on its masthead. The magazine's online persona (www.videography.com)
is always a great way to keep up on the latest and greatest of the
high-end gear and techniques.

The hands-down leader in digital video movie production is *RES*
Magazine. The first and final word on the future of binary filmmak-
ing, and sponsor of the now infamous RESFEST (www.resfest.com),
Jonathan Wells' mighty tome is considered by many, (myself

included) to be *the* mouthpiece of the digital moviemaker. If you want to know what's really going on behind all the hype, pick up an issue and commit it to memory.

Supplement that with copies of the *Hollywood Reporter* (www.hollywoodreporter.com) and *Red Herring* (www.redherring.com) so you can keep up on the buzz in Tinsel Town and Silicon Valley respectively, and you've pretty much got it covered.

PIXEL JUICE

The real power of desktop production lies in the broad palette of tools, which can contribute elements to the final production. The ease of use of this environment must include connectability, system administration and management of peripheral devices, such as scanners, hard disks, tape drives, CD-ROMs, cameras, and any other gizmo that tickles your fancy.

I don't particularly like computers. They're great as far as tools go but a tool is just a tool. I can't ever remember a time when I went out to the garage and "played" with my Makita 110mm circular saw. With a top end of 11,000 rpm at 7.5 amps, it's every bit as cool, in its own electro-mechanical kind of way as any of my computers.

Tinkering and tweaking your computer system takes time and energy away from other, far more important endeavors. If a system takes you more than a couple hours to set up and get running then you have the wrong system. Some people are naive enough to think that it will get easier, but it never does, and the few dollars that you saved by going against conventional wisdom will haunt you for a long, long time.

Once you embark on the binary path of digital production you automatically become a computer dweeb. Even if you're a card-carrying Luddite and don't intend on using a computer for titles, graphics, effects or even editing, the camera is a computer peripheral. It records binary data. The friendlier your computer system is, the better your life will seem.

It is precisely for this reason that I have seldom considered the Windows environment as a viable production alternative. I have two friends who love their Matroxes and one of my production associates has a D-Vision which we've used on several jobs with quite satisfactory results, but all three of them are full-on techno-weinies and love to tinker with their computers.

I use my own IBM IntelestationNT quite often for software applications that don't run on the Mac like Maya, SoftImage and Studio3D. My beloved palmtop is a Windows-based David of Goliath proportions. For high bit-depth and ultra-high resolution film projects I fire up the Silicon Graphics Workstation. The bottom line is that when it comes down to moving digital video around, nothing even comes close to a Macintosh.

The most articulate justification for platform choice that I've ever come across is from one of the most intelligent and creative people in the motion picture industry. It can be found at (www.apple.com/applemasters/mcrichton).

Price point is the king here. The cost-effectiveness of modern production tools is quite literally re-inventing communications on a global scale. One of the main characteristics of digital technology is how it blurs the lines of previously disparate endeavors. One box

77

can make commercials, motion picture effects, music videos, CD-ROMs, Web design, corporate videos... it's endless. The most important factor in picking the system that's right for you is the Cost/Resolution Factor.

PUTTING THE PEDAL TO THE METAL

'Nough theory, let's start designing your production environment. From Hi-Def to DV the choices and costs are endless. Like any determination regarding major investments, you want to make your decision based on which price performance ratio is best for you. The following chart is intended as an aid to help you determine your platform preferences.

	RESOLOUTION	SAMPLING	COLOR	DATA RATE	COMPRESSION	CAMERA PRICE
HUMAN BRAIN	3,000+ LINES	4:4:4	16+BIT	1GBS	DEPENDS	-----------
FILM	4,000+ LINES	4:4:4	20+BIT	1GBS	NONE	@$10,000
D-5	1080 LINES	4:2:2	10BIT	500+MBS	NONE	-----------
HD-CAM/24P	1080 LINES	4:2:2	10BIT	500+MBS	LOW	@$100,000
DVCPRO-HD	1080 LINES	4:2:2	10BIT	100MBS	6.7:1	@$60,000
D-1	525 LINES	4:2:2	10BIT	50MBS	NONE	-----------
DIGITALBETA	525 LINES	4:2:2	10BIT	50MBS	2:1	@$45,000
DVCPRO-50	525 LINES	4:2:2	8BIT	50MBS	3.3:1	@$40,000
DVCPRO	525 LINES	4:1:1	8BIT	25MBS	4.1:1	@$12,000
MINI-DV	525 LINES	4:1:1	8BIT	25MBS	5:1	@$3,000
NTSC-TV	480 LINES	-----	8BIT		-----	-----------

This chart is only an approximation, as prices and specifications change constantly.

When Is the Right Time to Buy?

We've all done it, wanted something but felt we should wait until the newest version comes out. The huge advances in technology are behind us. This is the post-digital age, a time when technology starts getting simpler to use and harder to see. This could be called the age of technological ubiquity, but that's an awfully pretentious title for a simplified paradigm. We need to start taking this technology for granted and focusing on what it can do for us. We need to start focusing on the methodology and less on the technology.

So when is the right time to buy? Answer: When you need it.

While we're on the topic of price performance... **Gordon Moore**, co-founder of Intel, hypothesized back in 1972 that the speed and performance of computer technology would double every two years while the size and price would halve. This formula has proved extremely accurate and is used almost unanimously in the computer industry as a basic rule of thumb.

For illustration, if the automobile industry performed at the same level today's Mercedes sedan, which in 1972 cost around $10K, would cost $0.12, get 10,000 mpg and travel near the speed of light. With the industry-wide acceptance of digital, the motion picture industry has just plugged into that formula. Hang on!

ASPECT WARS

The aspect ratio is the frame's width divided by its height. When movies started out they were almost square. Gradually they became wider to a point where they were roughly the same shape as a contemporary NTSC television signal, which is four to three, or 1.33:1. European and American cinema have been dueling back and forth about standards for quite some time. Europe adopted the 1.66:1 aspect ratio, and America the slightly narrower 1.85:1.

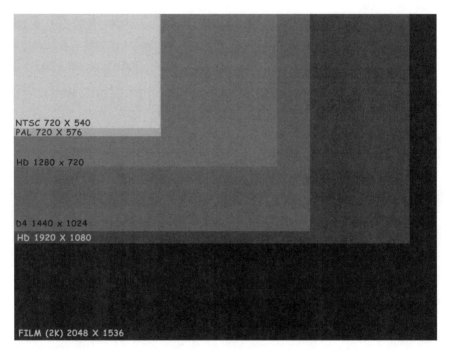

NTSC 720 X 540
PAL 720 X 576

HD 1280 x 720

D4 1440 x 1024
HD 1920 X 1080

FILM (2K) 2048 X 1536

There are of course many other aspect ratios that I have intentionally omitted. It's confusing enough.

NTSC television uses an aspect ratio of 4:3, an image four units wide and three units tall. Then along comes HDTV. Numerous size and resolution options have flown around since its initial introduction in the late '60s, and now, after more than thirty years of bickering, they've decided on a 16 x 9 aspect ratio.

The Net provides us with even more choices. Since the majority of compressors don't really care what the aspect ratio is, it's open season on format. While most sites prefer the conventional 4 x 3 of analog television, the new "virtual" formats — like i-View, QuickTimeVR and iPIX — offer a viewer-definable aspect ratio and framing environment.

The only thing I can say is that it's going to get even more confusing from here on out. Personally, I'm a 16 x 9 kind of guy.

Since the final image that we're aiming for is film, it will theoretically be projected in the widescreen aspect ratio of 1.85:1. The future of home television and video formats like HD, DVD and broadband lie in the realm of the 1.78:1 aspect ratio, usually referred to as 16 x 9. The majority of contemporary digital cameras now come with 16 x 9 aspect ratio capabilities. The better-quality systems generally use a wider chip with more horizontal pixels, while the majority of DV camcorders merely stretch or crop the image without really increasing the inherent resolution.

Let's say you've got a relatively unlimited budget for your project. You want to get the best video image possible so you've decided to shoot with the Panasonic AK-HC900 camera in 1080I/24p hooked directly

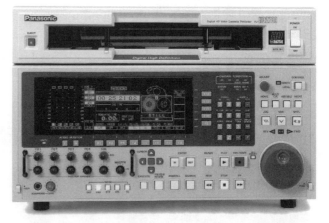

So actually this is a shot of the HD2700 that Panasonic lets me use occasionally. I haven't gotten up the nerve to borrow the 3700 yet. Maybe after the book is out.

into the Panasonic AJ-HD3700, D-5 HD Multi-Format Mastering VTR (my personal preference). This is the end of the video-for-film discussion, because by the time your image is printed, it will almost assuredly compare well to the vast bulk of conventional theatrical projections.

To most, this looks more or less like your basic high-end broadcast tape machine. It's not. The AJ-HD3700 records standard ITU-R 601 component video at 10 bits non-compressed using either 720 samples per line or 960 samples per line, for 16:9 recording with no resolution loss. It also records a variety of HD signals, including 24 and 25 frame progressive for cine work, in addition to more conventional 1080I and 720p HD images. Eight channels of audio are available in HD modes, 4 channels in standard definition mode. The HD3700 is a full-resolution recording system that employs a minimum motion-JPEG compression system to eliminate artifacts sometimes visible in other compressed HD recorders.

If, like me, you prefer a little grain in your image, there is a nice little plug-in filter set that can emulate the grain structure of Kodak's 45, 48, 93, and 96 film emulsions. I'm still waiting for the 5393 pushed to ASA400 filter. A D-5 tape, storing full-resolution

Dear Santa: I've been really, really good this year....

high-definition television 10-bit recording will give you 45 minutes of recording for less than $100. The D-5HD system can record up to 154 minutes at 24 frames, (2 hours' running at 1080I/60p) on a standard D-5 tape for under $300.

Now let's say that your budget is not necessarily less limited, but rather, you need the added convenience of a camcorder. The Sony-HDWF900 is a Multi-Format, HDCAM Camcorder featuring 24/25/30 frames per second progressive and 50/60 interlaced recording modes. Panavision has created its own version of this camera, complete with Panaflex lenses and a Panavision viewfinder. Given unlimited choices, I'd still rather burn film, but the distance between shooting emulsion and digital has been closed substantially. For the digital moviemaker, this is as good as it gets. When something comes out that is significantly better than the Panavision/Sony-HD camcorder, I'll write a new book.

I believe that the best thing that could happen to us as digital moviemakers would be for Sony to buy out Panavision and start kicking out modular, 10-bit, 4:2:2 mini-DV camcorders with really great glass, that shoot in native 16:9 and

More than just hardware, these cameras represent a new era in cinematic production.

are switchable between a wide variety of speeds. Just a thought.

Next step down the budgetary pathway leads to the land of compression schemes and 4:2:2 sampling. While there are more flavors arriving daily, the two most outstanding performers in this category are the Panasonic DVCPRO-HD with a data rate of 100 Mbps and the Panasonic DVCPRO50 at 50 Mbps.

My good friend Tony Salgado (www.24-7dtv.com) is a well-respected cinematographer who's had a substantial amount of experience with both film and video formats. Being a former co-conspirator in the never-ending battle of PAL for film use, his wisdom far exceeds my own when it gets down to the technical nuances of particular HD production environments.

On a recent electronic feature, Tony used Panasonic's AJPD-900WP, DVCPRO50, 16:9-480 Progressive Camcorder equipped with Canon high-definition lenses. As he explains it, "The benefits of 480p are that progressive recording allows increased vertical resolution and the absence of interlace motion and detail artifacts. Since the full-frame images are exposed at 1/60 of a second, you get a much sharper image when compared to interlaced. The other great thing is that it allows me to use existing SDTV support equipment and infrastructure."

During a 35mm film screening of footage Tony had acquired on the 480p system, several major high-definition facility personnel believed they were watching high-definition-originated material. Personally, I've seen a lot of film-based footage that had a far less cinematic look to it. Check out his site for some downloadable frames.

In addition to generating stunningly film-like images, the 480p system is usually less expensive to rent and far less expensive to own than a comparable DigitalBetacam system. As Tony is quick to point out, "With all the money you save on buying a 480P system you can afford to buy a really good, high-definition lens, especially important if you ever upgrade to an HDTV camera package."

I wanted to put a shot of my friend Tony in here with his tricked-out camera, but he was out on location by the time I got around to illustrations, so this offering from Panasonic of the AJ-HDC20 will have to do.

If you're purchasing your production system rather than renting, Panasonic's HD-150 Studio VCR provides an excellent upward migration path to High-Definition at a later date. Less expensive than a top-of-the-line DigitalBetacam recorder, it will play back numerous tape formats including DV, DVCPRO, DVCPRO50, 480P, as well as 1080I and 720p.

Panasonic also offers a new HD recording system in the DVCPRO line that performs pretty much the same as the Sony HDCAM system but at lower prices. DVCPRO-HD is an example of how HDTV is becoming ever more practical and affordable as an alternative to shooting on film.

Even when a recording that originated in progressive mode is played back as down-converted NTSC, the interlaced images still maintain noticeable improvement in terms of reduced edge artifacts and chroma dot crawl.

If the world of 4:2:2 is out of your reach and the esoteric realm of progressive scan is too spooky for you, then consider the high-end of the 4:1:1 category, the Sony DSR300. With 800 lines of 4:1:1 resolution sampled at 10-bit and an impressive 62db signal-to-noise ratio, this system creates the best signal in the entire 4:1:1 line. The increased bit-depth translates to a significantly better retention of color information. In many instances (up-conversion, chroma-key & visual effects) the 4:1:1, 10-bit signal out-performs many 4:2:2, 8-bit signals.

Sometimes you've got to take a look at the big picture to figure out what is really going to work best for your specific application. The best bang for the buck in video-for-film production today is BetacamSP. Yes, I know it's an analog acquisition system, but keep in mind that analog is analogous to infinite, while digital is fixed. Color-space digitizing schemes don't transpose well from one format to another.

In many instances, shooting in analog and then digitizing at your highest data rate will give you much better results in color-space. Since everyone in production is so polarized to everything digital, there are many golden opportunities awaiting the savvy moviemaker in the analog world. An aggressive and innovative person could conceivably put together a good used BetacamSP system that would drastically out-perform many, if not all of the prosumer quality DV-cam systems for a similar budget.

Keep in mind that one of the major factors in the inherent quality of the image comes from the quality of the lens. An industrial-quality BetacamSP lens is many times superior to consumer lenses, while a broadcast-quality BetacamSP lens is almost immeasurable.

My undisputed pick of the litter is the Sony BVW-D600 BetacamSP. Sony ImageWorks recently did a test: They up-converted the BVW-D600 image and printed it to film. The projected test was far more film-like and had a far more pleasing image than a comparable test done with DigiBeta.

So, you don't really have a budget after all? But hey, you did just get approved for a Discover card and now you see in the paper that Costco is running a special on mini-DV camcorders. All right, you're going to make a movie, dude! Now normally I'd tell ya' to stay away from the 4:1:1 consumer stuff because the color-space just isn't there and the lenses are all soft. But you've got your mind set on doing it and, after all, the important thing is to just get out there and start shooting.

Doesn't really matter which of the 4:1:1 systems you use; they're all going to give you basically the same thing. If you want to spend energy stressing over advertising hype, well then be my guest. The reality is that, at that resolution, a chip's a chip. The true limiting factor is the lens. Don't be fooled by the ability to change lenses. They're all still just prosumer quality, interchangeable lenses. At least get a camcorder that allows you to override the auto functions.

There is, however, one exception, and it comes from a recognized leader in lens manufacturing. The PAL version of the Canon XL-1 is called the XM-1 (www.canon.co.uk/). It costs about $1,000 more but is designed around the same professional modular approach that allows the user to change lenses. The truly hip thing about this camera is that it lets you shoot in 25fps, progressive, and has an anamorphic setting that actually compresses the image horizontally. When Fire Wire'd to your lossless edit suite and decompressed into true 16 x 9 aspect, you have the best quality DV image possible for printing to film from the mini-DV cams.

The important point to keep in mind is that the XM-1's supplied lens is on par with all the other mini-DV lenses. What you need to truly elevate the inherent quality

Like I said, mini-DV is all the same unless you dress it up all nice and professional.

of the video signal is a quantifiably superior lens and viewfinder system.

Ikegami stepped up to the plate and knocked one out of the park with their professional-quality B&W viewfinder. A good lens doesn't do you much good if you can't tell what you're shooting. Color viewfinders are nifty enough if you're grabbing some vacation shots or home movies (don't even get me started on those little flip-out, flat-screen, doohickeys), but they don't carry enough information to make the critical, on-the-spot decisions that justify using a high - quality lens in the first place.

All professional cameras from HD on down use black and white viewfinders. Any veteran cameraperson will tell you that you just can't get a critical focus with a color image because the color tricks the eye. Most likely, in the very same breath, this person will spew on about a personal hatred of auto-focus. Which brings us to the other really cool addition to Canon's little powerhouse, the mechanical lens. No auto-focus, no image stabilization, no power zoom, in fact nothing to degrade the video image outside of the limited bandpass of the mini-DV format itself. The lens is composed of fully coated glass elements and offers an unusually crisp image through its entire 14x focal range. (See actual comparisons in the TEST section of the PixelMonger website.)

Plop the viewfinder and mechanical lens onto your Canon XM-1 and you've actually got a professional production tool that will help you wrangle the very most out of your 4:1:1 mini-DV format. Figure around $4,000 for the finder and lens (www.videosmith.com) and you're now in a position to really do some damage.

Keep in mind that 90 minutes of PAL will actually run 93 minutes at 24fps so you'll need to stretch the audio track 4.16% to match. Other than that, try shooting at a shutter speed of 1/12th second to see if you like the effect (test), and don't use the camera's onboard mic. With this set-up, careful adherence to established production methodology, and a direct-digital laser print, your final image quality has the potential to match or surpass content originated on 16mm film. What more could you possibly want?

THE BOTTOM LINE

Whatever format or tools you end up using to shoot your epic, the two most important things to remember are: Try not to waste people's time, and don't burn bridges. Keep in mind that a wide market of distribution alternatives awaits the low-resolution moviemaker in the rapidly growing market of the Internet. Even if you don't end up with the high-caliber content that you originally envisioned, sites like my own (www.PixelMonger.com), www.shortbuzz.com, www.alwaysi.com, www.ifilm.com, www.inetfilm.com, www.bijoucafe.com, www.honkworm.com, www.mediatrip.com, www.undergroundfilm.com, and the always popular www.atom-films.com offer up distribution mechanisms for a wide spectrum of downloadable and streaming movies and are even more accessible to your market than taking the festival route.

TOP 10 TECHNICAL CONSIDERATIONS

Here are my top 10 technical particulars that could help you maximize your cost/resolution factor.

1.   If you're serious about shooting in digital video and then up-converting and printing to film, give serious consideration to building a PAL system. Computers and software don't care. Basically any format in PAL will out-perform the same format in NTSC in both resolution and color-space. There is simply 30% more data going to each frame at the film printer from images originating in PAL.

2.   Sometimes you can buy a used ENG system like BetacamSP for the same price as a spiffy new DV cam. What you'll get is a robust system that was built for professional use. The uncompressed signal will look much better when digitized into your desktop edit environment than re-compressing the

already 5:1 compressed DV signal. Just about any of the BetacamSP family of cameras has really nice CCDs that give a better tonality and a more filmic look than the tiny DV chip sets ever could.

3.   Learn the difference between 4:1:1 and 4:2:2, and then apply that knowledge to all future decisions.

4.   If you can't afford an Inferno on an SGI then get a Macintosh. I have, and use, top-of-the-line UNIX, WindowsNT and MacOS systems. Nothing moves video as well as a Mac.

5.   Shoot everything in 16 x 9.

6.   Digitize only once! Don't import something with FireWire or Targa and then re-compress it so you can use it on your Avid. Look out a window. Look out a window with a screen on it (digitized). Now, go get another screen and hold it in front of the window with the screen already in it (re-digitized). If you actually did this, the rippled pattern that you would see is called a moiré. Get it?

7.   The optimum methodology for doing effects is to shoot on film, then have it telecined to ITU-R 601 and archived to a Metrum for transport to your system. After you've done your thing on the desktop, cut it with the rest of your footage in the nonlinear environment. If you're using the desktop for off-line only, put your shots back on your transport system and have the post house transfer them to your production format. The important thing is to make sure your effects are put through the same hoops as your video.

8.   The best inexpensive video-to-film methodology is to shoot on BetacamSP and digitize (component) into your nonlinear. Keep everything on the same system and don't recompile your data files. When you're done take your computer and your hard drives over to a lab that has a Panasonic D5 and output in component to the D5. And use a company that has a laser printer and a lot of experience with pixel jockeys.

9.   My "pick-up" system consists of a very small Canon XM-1 DV (see figure, page 88) camera with FireWire into a Mac. (For prosumer video-to-film applications I recommend getting a full turnkey system from ProMax Technology (www.ProMax.com), or Intelligent Media Productions (www.intelligentmedia.com) for streaming media applications). Keep in mind that DV is only 4:1:1 so if you're looking to do visual effects (i.e., you need more color information), go back to #3.

10.   The price/performance leaders at this time, in my order of preference are:
      (A)   Panasonic AK-HC900 / AJ-HD3700, D-5 in 1080P
      (B)   Sony HDWF900PAC Multi-Format, HD Camcorder at 143MB Mbps
      (C)   Panasonic DVCPR-HD, 4:2:2 color sampling at 100 Mbps
      (D)   Panasonic DVCPRO50/480p, 4:2:2 color sampling at 50 Mbps
      (E)   Sony DSR300 800 lines of 4:1:1, DigitalBetacam
      (F)   Sony BVW-D600 — analog BetacamSP
      (G)   Canon XM-1 with manual lens and B&W finder

Who would ever believe that desktop production would get this outta control? The Apple/Pinnacle/Sony HD production station.

Notice how this list is so nicely split up and balanced between the two big guys, with Canon bringing up the rear. If we were to create a list of high-end, three-chip, prosumer camcorders, Canon would lead the list, with alternate Panasonic and Sony products falling in line below. If you don't get the subtext of this delicate arrangement, go back and reread the first chapter.

Acquisition is only half the battle. While the bulk of the higher res-olution platforms are still better served using their dedicated con-ventional postproduction environments for the online, there is a notable emergence of high-resolution, desktop solutions. One of the more popular of these tools is the HD Macintosh/Pinnacle system (www.pinnaclesys.com). Based around the 64-bit TargaCine card and utilizing Apple's own Final Cut Pro production application (www.apple.com/finalcutpro), the system offers a true 16:9 environ-ment with YUV processing, which eliminates the luma and chroma clamping issues that plagued earlier users.

The TargaCine's break-out box (page 54) comes with composite, component, S-video and SDI connections as well as eight channels of audio at 20-bit/48KHz. The 1/2 Terabyte of massively fast stor-age provides ample resources for the bulk of production scenarios. Weighing in at under $20,000 for the entire HD system, we are truly witnessing the emergence of a new era in moviemaking as these tools continue to get cheaper and more powerful with every week that passes.

In the end, many of your choices will be dictated by your budget. Or, in the immortal words of Randolph Bourne, "He who mounts a wild elephant goes where the wild elephant goes."

DIGITAL CINEMATOGRAPHY

I started my somewhat eclectic career in cinema as an assistant to Academy Award-winning cinematographer James Wong Howe (*Hud, The Rose Tattoo, The Molly Maguires*). Mr. Howe's acerbic wit and rough mannerisms made him an interesting person to work for. He died in the middle of shooting *Funny Lady* with Barbara Streisand and James Caan (talk about lighting the difficult two-shot).

Before his death I often took him to an acupuncturist out in the San Fernando Valley. As we were sitting there one day waiting for his appointment, a chiropractor from the adjoining office came bursting into the waiting room with a gurney full of what was then state-of-the-art video equipment. He proceeded to play his grainy, jittery, B&W home video for us until Mr. Howe turned to me and asked. "Scotty, you know why video always looks so crappy?" Well, I proceeded to ramble on about resolution and sample rates until he interrupted me. "Video," he said, "always looks so crappy 'cause there's so many crappy people shooting it." May he rest in peace.

Although harsh, he was actually quite correct in his observations. The most unfortunate aspect of digital cinematography is that it generally ends up looking like home video. If you don't particularly want your project to end up looking crappy, then treat your bantam-weight video camera as if it were a film camera.

A Canon XL1 dressed up like the big boys and ready to tango. Body brace, follow focus and mattebox by Karl Horn at (www.cinetechonline.com).

TAKE STOCK IN YOUR IMAGE

I'm sure it goes without saying that you should only use new, high-grade, brand-name videotape. Never re-use or tapeover anything, and keep it as dry and cool as possible. The tiny DV format tapes are far more delicate than you might imagine, especially after they have been recorded. Just remember that no matter how small they make the tape, it is still just rust glued onto plastic. However desperately we want to believe that this is the glorious digital age, we've got to remember that the vast majority of digital marvels are still composed of moving parts. Make dubs of your masters immediately and only use the masters for transfer or final online. 'Nough said.

GETTING THAT FILM LOOK

I'm not talking about the software filters here; we'll get to them later. I'm talking about the collective characteristics of the image that tell the audience whether they're watching a quality film production or another crappy video. The camera is the tool by which we record the story we are telling. The more professionally it is recorded, the more inherent perceived quality our production will have.

While both film and video record light reflected off of objects, they do it in different ways. Film is its own recording mechanism and storage medium, while video's image must be encoded and recorded to videotape, hard disk or RAM. Digital video is quite finite in its inherent form, while film possesses an almost infinite spectrum of attributes.

To get video to look like film we must develop methodologies that emulate the essential nuance of that medium. If we compare a single frame of 35mm film stock to a broadcast-quality video frame we will discover four main areas of difference.

First is the resolved size of the image. While an NTSC video frame has essentially 349,920 pixels (720 x 486), a frame of film is easily capable of resolving 12,582,912 pixels (4,096 x 3,072).

The amount of color that a medium records is called the colorspace or color gamut. Film can display over 800 million colors while the best uncompressed video can barely maintain a color gamut of 256 colors for each of its three component colors. Red=256, Green=256 and Blue=256, which, when cubed, gives us 16.7 million colors. And for every color video can display, film can display 48.

97

As we will discuss later in the chapter, film has a much higher contrast ratio (dynamic latitude) than video and can record more than six times the range of illumination. This gives film far more depth and detail as highlights roll off gently into denser regions. The same scene on video would generate solid blotches of black or white.

The fourth, and perhaps most subjective difference is grain. It is that almost subliminal signature that tells us we are watching something of inherent value. Grain gives texture to the image and makes it more interesting.

The following suggestions will help you keep your video image from looking like video. Whether or not you can tell a good story, well, that's up to you.

Dynamic Motion

Film cameras are generally bulky, heavy affairs. When they move, it is generally with a plodding massiveness that belies their inertia. Video camcorders on the other hand are light, flimsy affairs that we can fling around with mindless abandon.

Go rent your top ten favorite movies, brew a big pot of coffee and get yourself a yellow pad. Now, watch all ten movies and make note of every time the camera flits around or makes any movement that could in any way be construed as coming from an object weighing in at under thirty pounds.

Lightweight camcorders were designed for home video use. If you want your image to move like it came from a film camera, create an environment that causes your tiny camcorder to move like a real film camera. If you're going to use a tripod, get a big one with a large fluid head. Get something that was built to hold a fifty-pound camera, and it will give you moves that echo that massive environment.

For handheld shots go get yourself a ten-pound weight at the local sporting goods store, or better yet get someone to machine something cool for you — and hook that little, flimsy camcorder to it and leave it there. It will give your shots a massiveness and inertial quality that is nearly impossible with a camcorder.

Motion Artifacts

The motion artifacts of video are unique and tell an audience that they are watching video even after you've printed to film. If you shot your movie on a PAL system, the artifacts will be far less noticeable as having originated on video, but they'll still be annoying. Bright objects moving horizontally across the frame and fast camera pans are the worst. Serious testing is in order if you're considering such movements.

Image Stabilization

While we're on the topic, don't buy a camera that has image stabilization; if you are forced to use a camera that has it, never turn it on. This is a feature best relegated to tipsy wedding photographers and harried vacationers. If you can't hold your camera still, put it on a tripod and cut down on the caffeine.

Image stabilization in prosumer camcorders essentially works by fixing on an area of high contrast and then stretching the image and taking just the middle part. The decrease in resolution and sharpness is unacceptable in professional video, much less in video that is destined to be printed on film.

Nix the Zoom

One of the biggest tip-offs that you're watching video is a zoom. DON'T ZOOM! DON'T EVER ZOOM! It doesn't matter whether or not you think a zoom will enhance the end result! Go back and look at your top ten movies again. You can probably use the same sheet on your yellow pad. Not a "dolly" or a "truck" or a "push" where the camera actually moves closer to the subject. I'm talking zoom. After viewing all ten of your favorite movies please notice how nice and clean your yellow pad is.

Zooms are for weddings and home video. Filmmakers on the other hand, generally use a very expensive set of prime lenses or at least the metaphor. A "prime" is a lens of fixed focal length. In DP lingo it refers to the distance between the optical center of the lens and the film plane, when the lens is focused at infinity (endless point in space, not the car). To the videographer it means that you frame the shot using the zoom function selecting a setting between "wide" and "telephoto," and then leave it there as you make your shot.

If you need to get the actor's face to fill the scene, get up off your ass and physically move closer. The object is to move the camera. A camera move gives a scene dynamics and a greater sense of presence. It helps develop a point of view and establishes the environment in which you're telling the story. Yes, there are professional zoom lenses but they are generally used as a rapidly accessible set of prime lenses.

While we're on the topic of lenses, I'd like to offer up an observation. The tendency with small video camcorders is to get too close to the subject. They're small and unobtrusive, almost ubiquitous in contemporary society. Add to this the high number of people who are using a camera-mounted microphone, and it's probably safe to say that this is one of the bigger factors in the "video" look. The problem with shooting someone from a short distance is that you'll generally need to use a rather wide lens that has an angle of view in excess of 90 degrees. People tend to look goofy when shot with wide-angle "short" lenses. A lens that has an angle of view in the 10-degree range will generally put you at least 12 feet away from the subject and generally give you a far better sense of the person's character. Test this as often as it takes till you get the feel.

CHOOSING A CAMERA

Automatic anything is bad. First thing you need to look for in the selection of an appropriate digital video camcorder is whether or not you can override the automatic functions. Auto-focus, auto-iris, auto-white balance, these functions are created for amateur home videoists, not digital moviemakers.

If you can't override the auto functions of your camera, stop here, put the book down and go do something else, because anything you shoot is going to look bad and drag us all down. The unmistakable shift as the auto-focus searches for something to lock onto, or the nauseating displacement in depth of field as the auto-iris corrects for changes in brightness — these are all the unmistakable signatures of cheap video, indicating that whatever follows should not be taken seriously.

Mattebox

The camera is a system designed to collect and control a stream of reflected light within the limits of its designated recording specifications. Perhaps the most practical and significant step towards controlling light is the mattebox lightshade. It serves a dual purpose, as its name would suggest — of shading the forward lens element from stray shafts of light, while also allowing you a mechanism for attaching a variety of filters. You'd be hard-pressed to find a professional film or video camera that didn't sport one of these most basic tools of the trade.

My baby in "serious" mode.

The sorry attempt for a shade that accompanied your camcorder doesn't count, and whether you construct one yourself out of cardboard or spring for one of those custom, after-market jobs, there is little you can do to improve the quality of the image. To be effective the shade should extend at least six inches from the front element, and be solid enough so that it doesn't wiggle around.

Checking for Cut-Off

To make sure the mattebox's occlusion is as close to the image edge

102

as possible without impinging, put your finger at the center of the four sides and move it in toward the center until it shows up in the viewfinder. Your finger should be just short of the first joint. Any less and you run the chance of the mattebox cutting into the image; any more and you won't get the full light shading benefits.

Gain

Most cameras have a gain switch that increases the camera's sensitivity in low-light situations. When you increase the gain, you add noise to the image, which in some instances looks a bit like the grain found in a fast film emulsion. Many people use the gain setting as a shortcut to lighting. Don't!

True, a little grain is the fastest way to add that cinematic nuance to your video image, but there are far better ways to do this in post. What you lose by boosting gain in the acquisition stage is resolution, color space and the ability to control the amount of grain you end up with in your final print. What might seem like teeny-tiny little specks of grain on your video monitor will look like a full-on blizzard after printing to film. Once it's in your image, it's almost impossible to get out. A drop of super glue is the best thing you can do to your gain switch. That way you'll never be tempted to use it.

VIDEO LEVELS

On the other end of the scale is the problem of too much light. When shooting video that will later be printed to film you should avoid shooting in direct sunlight when possible. The contrast ratio generated by direct sunlight is far greater than most video cameras can handle, and the resulting image problems are only worsened in the printing process. Contrast isn't such a big deal if you're staying in a pure video environment, but you must always keep in mind that you're heading for film. Contrast gained in the acquisition stage is only going to worsen as you progress.

Most professional video cameras have a mechanism known as the *zebra indicator,* which lets the operator know if there are areas of illumination within the scene that exceed the camera's ability to record it. Wherever the brightness exceeds the pre-set level, the zebra indicator superimposes a striped pattern over the area.

The zebra is generally based on a setting of 80 to 95 IRE (Institute of Radio Engineers). Think of 0 IRE as total black and 100 IRE as total white, indicating the maximum amount of voltage that the system can handle. While film can quite often record these values, NTSC video considers black at 7.5 IRE units (usually called the *pedestal*

The clouds in this shot are too hot to handle and display the "Zebra" pattern to warn of clipping.

in postproduction and *set-up* in the field), and peak white at 80 to 95 IRE. If you can set your zebra indicator to start clipping at 70 to 75 IRE you will be able to maintain detail in the brightest areas of your finished film. If you push it into the 90 to 95 IRE level, the brightest areas of your finished film will be little more than splotches of light with little or no image information in them.

At the lower end of the contrast problem are the blacks. Just as the high-intensity whites will have a tendency to *blow out* when printed to film, so will the blacks have a tendency to *crush* and go all black. The human eye is really the culprit here. We look at a scene and can make out the detail in the shadows just fine. Several months later we're sitting in a dark screening room arguing with our account executive about the huge black swaths of black that hide the subtle actions and details that we worked so hard to create.

Just because you can see it with the human eye, don't believe it. Just because you can still make it out on the video monitor, don't believe it. If you've got something going on in the shadows that you want the audience to share, make sure that information makes it to the screen by giving it far more illumination than you'd normally think it needs. A black that weighs in at between 9 to 10 IRE will give you very pleasant, uncrushed shadows by the time you get to the screen.

By keeping a close eye on the contrast ratios that you're creating within your scenes, you should hopefully arrive at the film printer with a slightly flat-looking video master. Of course you've tested all this beforehand, right?

A waveform monitor should always be the final arbitrator of the lighting values in your video image. It determines what is "broadcast quality" by measuring the actual voltages of the video image and is often the first indication that your image is destined to have problems when printed to film.

A waveform monitor measures the level of the video signal as voltage, and is capable of representing the image visually in several forms. The most common use of the waveform monitor is to monitor the pedestal and peak white levels of the video image.

Waveform monitor and vectorscope pumping color bars off tape.

Most software applications and nonlinear edit platforms also have built-in signal diagnostics. These slightly more sophisticated systems generally include a vectorscope as well, which is helpful in determining the color timing of your video signal. They may be a bit more accurate only because of their sophisticated software/hardware compression schemes, but to truly quantify and calibrate your camera, you need to run the video through a real, honest-to-goodness, physical waveform monitor. This is the only way you can really start to visualize what your signal is actually doing.

Latitude

Motion picture film is able to record a significantly greater range of light intensity than video. While the average motion picture film stock can generally accommodate at least a ten-stop range (Kodak figures film at 1,000:1 contrast ratio) in the brightness of a scene, prosumer video is good for only a fraction of that if it's lucky (Kodak figures video at 150:1 contrast ratio). A really good, professional camcorder like a D-Beta or DVCPRO50 may get as much as seven stops, but it is still in a limited gray scale resolution. The method with which the video industry calculates a particular camera's response to light is expressed in terms of *range* and graphically represented by the *response curve*.

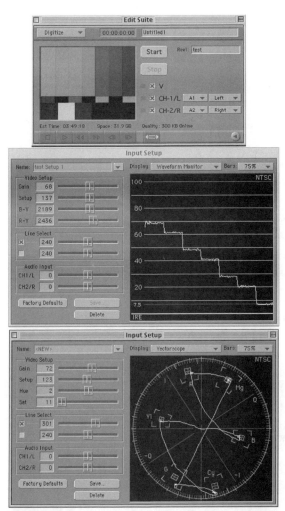

Software-based signal analysis. Although convenient and widely accepted, I still don't trust them like I do my Tektronix.

The human eye can perceive an enormous range in the levels of brightness. Standing inside a house at night our eyes can make out details both within the brightly-lighted interior

107

of the house as well as in its dark and shadowy exterior. A fast motion picture film would struggle with a high-contrast lighting environment like this, while any video format would fail miserably.

KODAK 5248 ASA 100 FILM STOCK

SONY DSR-500WS DVCAM

Film is not only more forgiving with high-contrast ratios, but also handles the way the extreme values of white and black are handled. While video essentially *clips* the values that exceed its limits, film has a far more forgiving nature. At the brightest and darkest ends of the scale of lumination, film eases the values into all white or all black. This is called the "soft shoulder."

In an attempt to soften the abrupt clip levels of video the *knee* compression circuit, or *soft clip* was devised. While it really doesn't do that much for the blacks, it has the capacity to noticeably extend the exposure range by emulating the soft shoulder of film. Many cameras have circuitry that reduces contrast by averaging the signals. While this often creates better-looking video, it isn't recommended for video destined for film due to the amount of information that is discarded in the equation.

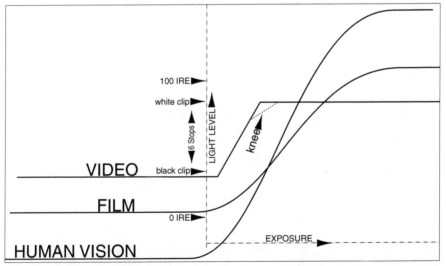

In many cameras the angle of the knee-compression circuit can be adjusted and lengthened to give even greater exposure range. With careful calibration the range of a high-quality camera can be expanded almost two *f* stops.

109

LENSES

Unfortunately there is no such thing as a perfect lens. They all suffer from varying degrees of chromatic aberration, diffraction, slight variances in the index of refraction, and low-tolerance manufacturing anomalies. Generally a glass lens is far superior to a resin one, and a coated lens is always superior to an uncoated one. The more elements (individual lenses) a system has, the greater the resolving power and accuracy. The essential quality of a lens can be expressed in terms of f stop or T-factor.

The quality of cinematic lenses like a nice Cook Prime or the always-popular Panaflex, is far, far, far superior to that of any prosumer camcorder. There is an unsubstantiated rumor that the video camera manufacturers actually de-engineer the camcorder lenses so that they don't compete with their far more expensive ENG (Electronic News Gathering) systems. Comparing them side by side generates a compelling argument for these rumors, since the CCDs are often quite similar.

So there you are, starting out with inferior glass, or plastic, as the case may be. Compounding the deficiencies in light gathering, focus and image sharpness is the fact that virtually all camcorders come with zoom lenses, which further degrades the already insubstantial image quality.

The solution is to either use a professional camcorder that takes professional quality lenses, or use the sweet spot of the lens you have built into your digital wonder. The sweet spot falls into a tiny bracket of functionality, and when adhered to faithfully can help overcome many of the physical inadequacies of the camcorder's optics. To find the sweet spot you must first have a rudimentary understanding of how the lens works.

Controlling the Flow of Light

By adapting standard cinematic methodologies to the digital video metaphor we will begin to create an ambiance, if not the actual resolution of studio-quality fare. By looking at how the camcorder handles light we can work around its limitations, and get a step nearer to creating that truly epic film-like look.

Exposure is the calculation of light intensity over time. Or, Exposure + Intensity x Time. Every increase or decrease in time or intensity will inversely affect the other in equal proportion. If you double the amount of light but decrease the amount of time by half, the exposure remains the same.

The *aperture* controls the amount of light allowed to pass through a lens. It is regulated by the *iris,* which looks and operates similarly to the iris in our own eyes. When shooting in low-light situations the iris opens up to allow more light to fall onto the CCDs. Similarly, a well-lit page of type is far easier to read than a poorly lit one.

The amount of opening of the iris is expressed as an f stop, which is a mathematical equivalent calculated by dividing the focal length by the effective diameter of the lens that is in use at that particular setting. A lower f stop opens up the aperture, allowing in more light and shortening the depth of field. With a wide open aperture an object that is in focus at five feet will have a "field of focus" extending only a few feet or even inches towards and away from the lens.

As the lens is "stopped down" and the iris is closed tighter, the amount of light hitting the CCDs is greatly reduced and the field of focus is extended. The same object that is in focus at five feet may have a field of focus that extends from just a few inches in front of the lens, out to infinity.

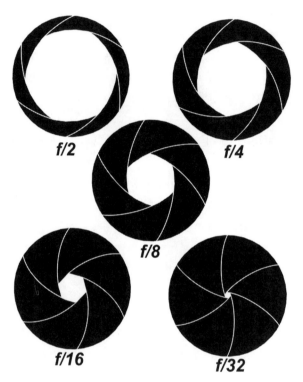

f/2

f/4

f/8

f/16

f/32

The wider the iris, the more light hits the CCD and the shorter the depth of field becomes.

The vast majority of camcorders don't have f stop indicators on their lenses, and in most cases attenuate the luminance value of the initial video signal to give an electrically arrived-at correlated f stop value. The f stop is usually displayed in the viewfinder window next to the shutter speed. If I thought that any of you'd really do it, I'd recommend going out and getting a high-quality light meter and then spend an entire chapter on how to use it. Nothing will give you consistently better composition and exposures. Failing that, you've got to become familiar with the manual control of aperture and shutter speed.

Shutter

The other way the lens/camera regulates light is the shutter. Film cameras have a physical shutter that cuts off the flow of light while the next frame of film is dragged forward. The standard motion picture shutter consists of a spinning disk with an opening of a specified angle that rotates at the frame rate of the film. A shutter that has an opening of 180 would be open half the time. Since the standard frame rate of cinema is 24 fps and the shutter is open half the time, the shutter speed would be 1/48 second. This is generally rounded off to 1/50 second in most film cameras.

Video CCDs, on the other hand, generate a steady stream of image/data. Since there are two fields to every frame, and NTSC

operates at 30 fps, most NTSC video cameras shoot at a shutter speed of 1/60 second. Many decent quality video cameras have an electronic shutter which will be able to give you shutter speeds from 1/4 second up to 1/10,000 second. The controls might not be obvious, so check your owner's manual.

This illustrates a 90-degree shutter, which would transpose to 1/100 second exposure.

Even though the camera is recording at

1/60 second, by setting the shutter at a lower rate, say 1/15 second, you start to develop a "look" that many people feel echoes the nuance of film more closely. Once you enter the realm of frame-rate experimentation, testing becomes imperative.

The object is to find an f stop that gives a good intermediate depth of field and maximizes the optical properties of your particular lens system, and then use that f stop to shoot your entire movie. Try starting with a shutter setting of 1/100 second, which would translate to a film shutter speed of 90. This will give your video frames just a bit more crispness than I personally like, but many people feel it creates a more film-like perception of individual pictures being run in sequence. A frame rate of 1/100 second works even better when using a PAL system.

You can also use the shutter to control the amount of light without changing your f stop or adding neutral-density filters. Each consecutive exposure time is cutting down or increasing the amount of light entering the camera by one f stop, which means that it is effectively halving or doubling the exposure. Don't go above 1/250 second without doing some tests to see if you like the strobing effect that it creates.

The Secret of Neutral Density

Since you've now got your trusty mattebox hooked up to your camcorder, you can easily attach neutral-density (ND) filters to it. These are plain gray filters that absorb light of all colors in equal amounts. Think of them as sunglasses for your camera. They are used to control the quantity of light that enters the lens, not the quality. You will need a small collection of these relatively inexpensive filters before you start shooting.

While you can spend hundreds of dollars on a really nice Tiffen glass set, for camcorder use a decent cut gelatin set is quite sufficient. Basically a ND 0.1 will allow 80% of the light through, which would increase your exposure by 1/3 f stop. The ND 0.6 reduces transmission by 25%, which is an even two f-stop increase. At the top of the practical collection would be the ND 0.9, which would result in a three f-stop increase, or 87% reduction in the amount of light entering the camera.

What we are trying to do here is stabilize and reduce the "low-light" sensitivity of the camcorder so that it begins to echo the light-handling characteristics of a conventional film camera. By throwing an ND over the lens we are forcing the scene to be lit just the same way you would be forced to light a conventional film set. Once you get your mind around this concept, and accept that it will entail far more work than simply turning on your automatic camcorder and shooting away, you will start to generate some truly filmic shots.

Polarizing Filter

Since light bounces around in all directions along its axis, the reflections that it creates in windows, water, and glass lenses often create an impenetrable barrier. A polarizing filter is an essential accessory that can reduce or eliminate these reflections. In exterior shots it can darken the sky and create far more dramatic clouds than you'd generally find.

In the most simplistic of terms, when light strikes a reflective surface like glass or water it becomes polarized and bounces in only one direction. Think of a polarizing filter as two pieces of glass or plastic with some microscopic venetian blinds laminated in between.

What these micro-blinds do is essentially filter out all of the random light and allow only the parallel-polarized light to pass. The object is not to eliminate all of the reflection but rather to reduce it to a point where it becomes a suggestion of reflectivity.

Polarizing filters are also used for penetrating haze, and in many cases make a good ND filter. While not as constant as a conventional ND, a good polarizer is generally good for a filter factor of ND 0.2 or 1-1/2 f stops. When shooting trees and foliage, a polarizing filter can raise the color saturation of leaves and shiny surfaces significantly by reducing their surface specularity.

Finding the Sweet Spot

You've got to experiment with your system to find its particular sweet spot. Short of buying a light meter, you'll need to buy, build, or steal some test charts. You'll need these for the rest of your illustrious career so plan on spending a little time or money on 'em. Everyone's got favorites, but since I transition between the worlds of film and video on a daily basis, I have a few recommendations and samples of this book's website at (www.pixelmonger.com) that are of particular relevance to the digital video-for-film community.

Go outside on a bright sunny day and shoot a few seconds of a person standing in full sunlight, utilizing all of the automatic functions of your spiffy new camcorder. Next, set up the 85% gray card in the same location and angle it so that sunlight is falling fully upon it. Now, turn off the auto functions of your camcorder. You will probably need to read the instruction manual of your particular camcorder to see how to override the auto-iris and auto-focus functions. The f stop equivalent on camcorders is generally displayed in a small LCD window within the viewfinder, and has a tiny button or dial for adjustment.

The idea is to place various densities of ND filters over your lens until you arrive at a good average setting that's good for shooting your entire production. I like *f*/8 because it gives me a nice depth of field, not too deep, not too shallow, and it is almost smack in the middle of any professional lens, which gives you plenty of room to move. I like to use combinations of the ND 0.2 because it matches the transmission index of most polarizing filters.

Once you're locked into a nice solid *f*/8 (5.6 to 11 will also do) have someone step in front of your gray card (you can use the blank gray page in the Color Plate section of this book). With the auto-focus feature on your camcorder disabled, perform a manual focus using the highlight in the eye as a point of focus. It is often helpful to zoom into the person's eye, focus and then zoom back out and re-frame the shot. This is the only time you're allowed to use the zoom!

The sharpest setting for most lenses is generally 1-1/2 to 2 stops down from the widest aperture, while the sharpest resolved image is obtained with the greatest depth of field using the smallest aperture. The method we're working with here should give us the best of both worlds.

Once you've got a good recording of your subject in full light, rig a white bed sheet, or better yet a section of a white Army-surplus parachute, above them so that the sunlight is diffused. Shoot a few seconds more of your subject. Next get a bright white surface at least several feet square, and position it to the side and slightly below the eye line of your subject. Make sure the surface is bouncing light back toward the subject's face. Record a few seconds of this. As simplistic as this exercise sounds, when you view the resulting images on a

117

video monitor you should notice a far more filmic look in the later shots than in your original one.

CAMERA PLACEMENT

Just because you see life at eye level, don't confine the camera there. This is not life, it's art. The placement of the camera is one of the most important acts in filmmaking. It is the statement of what the scene represents and of how the audience is supposed to view this particular situation.

Theater-going is not a democratic process. It's not supposed to be. You've got the sofa spuds that like to sit way back so the whole screen is close to the same size as their beloved television tube. You've got the sensation junkies who inhabit the first few rows, looking more for visceral interaction than insightful characters. Then you've got the rest of your audience. Me, I like twelfth row center. That's what the DP shoots for and whoever is sitting in that seat is essentially looking through the viewfinder.

Multiple Cameras

Get two cameras, set one on a tripod and handhold the other so one's over the shoulder and one's on the face for the close-up. There, you just saved a lot of time and energy. Heck, get three cameras. What does it matter, these things are cheap. The more coverage you get now, the more choices you'll have later. After you develop a rhythm with your actors you'll find that the first take's almost always the one with the magic. Generally you'd shoot a couple more takes, then come around for the close-up or the two-shot and do the series all over again.

But chances are, you're not using top-notch actors. Maybe they don't know how to modulate their performances, or they don't have the slightest understanding of re-creating the same performance you just shot from the side when you come around for the close-up. These mismatches in the flow of the performance might not look like much on the set, but by the time you get into editing they won't cut. Even if you do recognize the problem, the more you shoot, the more it'll just keep getting muddier and muddier, and you'll never get back the magic of that first take.

In conventional film production the whole process is so convoluted with DPs and their crews, loading, cleaning, checking, and logging each shot that hardly anyone ever uses multiple cameras. But hey, you're not using film. Cheapest thing you've got is videotape. Burn it up baby! By using multiple cameras you can cut the on-set time nearly in half. Since the actor knows that there are several angles being shot at once, they will want to put more effort into the portrayal.

And while we're on the topic of burning video, don't be foolish enough to try to save money by not running the tape a bit before and after takes. Heads and tails are very important. Just because you pressed the little red button doesn't mean that you're recording. Do it like the pros and let the tape get up to speed. Sure video starts up a lot faster than film, but it's always better to have a little extra than not enough.

Set-ups

All things being equal you should figure on an efficient production crew getting at least thirty to forty exterior set-ups a day. Interiors generally slow you down a bit because of the lighting. If they don't slow you down then you're not taking enough time lighting the scene.

Interiors

I personally like interiors, while perhaps the majority doesn't. I especially like sound stages where everything is designed for the process of getting the shot. Interiors allow you much greater control over continuity. When you're done shooting for the day simply shut off the lights and lock up. Next morning everything's in the same place, the lights are all the same value, the actor's marks are still where you left them. Don't have enough budget for a sound stage? Rent an old warehouse for a month or two. It not only gives you a place to build your sets but you can rig huge, stationary, soft boxes that can be used throughout your entire production.

Several years ago we shot *Barb Wire* in the old Hughes Helicopter factory out in Playa Del Rey. Funkiest old building you ever saw but it gave the cast and crew a home base to work out of as well as an inexpensive location for the movie's production. The look of the movie actually took on much of the look of the building. Many of the props were merely re-purposed materials we found lying around. It's not just funky, small budget projects that use old hangars and warehouses. During the same time we were in production, *Independence Day* was in preproduction in the even funkier adjacent building.

One of the big secrets to lighting a scene is to have plenty of room to move the lights and camera around. The more control you have over the light, the more control you have over the audience's perception of the scene. Bare bulbs focused directly at your actors create a harsh environment and amplify the agony or torment that they may be experiencing, while a collection of soft, diffused light sources create an atmosphere of peace and tranquillity. When you're setting your lights, don't forget to turn the house lights off!

WRANGLING THE BEAM

The actual type of light you use isn't nearly as important as how you control it, so rather than get involved in describing all the various flavors of lighting instruments available to the filmmaker, we'll look at some cost-efficient methods of wrangling the beam. Consider renting or buying a small lighting kit, nothing bigger than 1 kilowatt (kw) with several small focusable lights, a couple larger spots and a few soft lights such as KinoFlo or Chimeras.

There are essentially two main types of "key" light — raw sun and artificial light.

The "key" light is the main source used to light the subject, while the "fill" light generally comes from an angle close to the camera and is responsible for "filling in" and softening some of the shadows caused by the key light. The intensity of the key in proportion to the "fill light" determines the mood of the scene. A "high key" lighting set-up creates a bright scene with a lot of highlights, while a "low key" scene has a much higher ratio of lighting, and creates a much darker and visually more contrasting scene.

The basic rule of thumb states that the ratio of key light plus fill light should be 2:1 for prosumer video formats or as much as 3:1 in professional systems with higher resolving power. It's a good idea not to exceed 4:1 unless you're going for a particular look.

METERING THE SCENE

Let's say the first check cleared the bank and you're on a shopping binge. Consider saving a few hundred bucks by getting a camcorder with a few less bells and whistles, and then take the extra coins and buy yourself a nice light meter. I know I keep harping on this, but there is simply no toy, ahem, excuse me, piece of professional production equipment that you can purchase that will give you consistently better-looking images than a good meter. Falling short of that, learn to take readings with your camera.

It's not all that hard really, once you get used to it. The trick is to get used to it before you start shooting your movie. Have someone hold the gray card up to get the correct exposure for your actor's face and read the f stop off the indicator

Dollar for dollar, the best investment you can make is a good light meter. I have quite a few but this one is my favorite.

on your particular camera. Another rule of thumb says to stop down 1/2 stop for Caucasians, and open up 1/2 stop for darker skin.

Once you've got the scene and your actor metered, have the actor or the "stand in" stand in, and get up close and meter the darkest and then the lightest portions of the face. If the darker side of the face reads one stop higher than the bright side of the face, then you are at the recommended lighting ratio (2:1) for video that is to be printed to film. Always keep in mind that you're going to gain contrast when you print to film. If you do get to the final edit and determine that the shot is too flat, you can always boost the contrast; but if you shot it too "contrasty" to start with, you're stuck with it.

RAW SUN

The main advantages of sunlight over artificial light are that it is free, covers your entire scene and is quite easy to manipulate. The wide assortment of devices used for controlling and directing sunlight are generally far less expensive and easier to use than other forms of illumination.

While *direct* sunlight can be harsh in a filmed environment, in a video environment it's downright severe. The intensity of the sun's illumination isn't the only problem that it causes. It moves. Steadily and continuously the sun sweeps across the sky all day long. Shots you took in the morning sun won't always cut into shots at the same location later in the day.

If, like everyone else in the industry, you look at your dailies in the order shot, rather than sequentially, you probably won't see the problems until weeks or months later in editing. It is extremely noticeable when you spend several hours shooting someone's dialogue and then come around to shoot the other person's dialogue after lunch.

When you go back for reactions on the first actor you could have a gap of three or four hours. That amount of time span creates an enormous gap of believability. The audience may not know what's wrong but they'll know something's not right. While they've stopped to figure out what the problem is, they aren't following your story.

Perhaps the oldest and most widely used accommodation for mellowing out direct sunlight is cloud cover. Often called "God's silk," cloud cover generates a mellow, diffused light that records well on film or video. With film, this is generally all you need, but with video you should also introduce a bit of "fill" to keep your subject from going flat.

More important than the source of your light is how you control it. These simple tools allow you to diffuse, cut, bounce and generally mold the light to do your bidding. They are indispensable.

Fill panels are generally part of the gaffer's kit, but it's always good to have a couple of your own lying around. The two most common varieties are foam core art board, which can be picked up at any art store, and the more professional (and more costly) spring-loaded "hoops." The hoops generally have one side white and the other either metallic silver or gold.

When you don't have good cloud cover, or the clouds are small and sporadic, it's time to pull out the diffusion panel. You can buy these large panels of translucent material ready-made or make them yourself out of some PVC pipe and an old Army-surplus parachute.

The difference between a shot in direct sunlight and one done in diffused light is quite dramatic as you've seen if you followed directions earlier on.

The Spectrum of Light

The other problem with sunlight is that it changes color throughout the day. This is generally something that you can't see with the human eye unless it's sunset or sunrise. Imagine that you're shooting in a huge domed filter that is red at both horizons, bright yellow at the 45's and white "dead top center." Generally these types of color-density shifts are taken care of in the color-timing stage of a film's production. With digital video, this means that you've got to add another very time-consuming step to the processing of your images.

ARTIFICIAL LIGHT

Basically, light looks white to the human eye. That's because we have a mechanism in our brain that actually corrects for color shifts in the environment around us. It's actually rather unnerving when you realize how inaccurate the human eye is at determining color. Ever notice someone's window from outside at night when they're watching TV? It has an intense blue glow to it while the window right next to it may have a reddish cast and the one next to that golden.

From the street our brain will actually see the broad variations in color generated by various lighting mechanisms, because we don't have a lock on a specific color reference. If we were to walk into that house and into the room with the television in it, everything would appear quite normal. Our brain knows the inherent color scheme of the environment and corrects accordingly. As we move from room to room, the same location that we saw generating a reddish hue will also seem normal, as will the room with the golden cast.

With film we must constantly monitor the "color temperature" of lights. Many lights actually change color over time as the elements warm up, and corrective filters must be added. There are two main film types which are balanced to the light source frequencies of tungsten (code B at 3,200 K [Kelvin]) and Daylight (code D at 5,600 K). Scenes lit with sunlight will appear normal when using a film stock balanced for daylight, while scenes lit with 3,200 K studio lights will appear normal when shot on a film balanced for tungsten.

If you were using studio lights to enhance an outdoor scene that was using the sun as the key light, you would need to put blue "gels" over the lights to balance their color temperature. If you're shooting inside using studio lights as your key, then you would need to put orange gels over the windows to balance the natural sunlight coming in the windows. Many DPs in this situation will choose to shoot a daylight film and correct the key lights to daylight, or use a lighting source such as the neon KinoFlo.

In many instances you will find that various lights have different color temperatures. It is a good idea to actually videotape all of the locations that you plan on using at night, prior to starting production. Different lights will require "gels" to balance their color temperature. A fluorescent light next to an incandescent table light may create a noticeable and unwanted effect.

While there are tuned and tinted bulbs that can be placed in conventional sockets, the most common practice is to wrap fluorescent tubes with gels. Within a fixture it is also possible to have several neon tubes, each generating a wide range of color temperatures — from pink to bilious green. Needless to say, lighting is better done prior to the arrival of the non-gaff crew and actors.

White Balance

Unlike the human eye, the CCD is stupid. It translates what it is fed into electrical current which is encoded into a video signal. Video has an entirely different method for dealing with color temperature. It's called "white balance" and it's basically a modulator that shifts the frequency of the entire video signal up or down to accommodate for the ambient color of the environment.

On most prosumer camcorders the white balance is an automatic gizmo. Find out how to disable the auto functions and keep it off! Hopefully, your camera will have the capacity to set a white balance through the lens. If not, consider another camera.

Manually setting the white balance is actually quite simple and consists of placing a white board or piece of paper at the point at which your principals will be standing, and then focusing the camera at the target. Once the target fills the viewfinder, hit the white balance button, and the color reference of the camera will shift to accept your lighting set-up as white. If you want to add some colored filters to the scene for effect, do it after you've taken the white balance, or your filtered light will be balanced out.

Color Temperature

Color is expressed in terms of color temperature, and essentially ranges for our purposes between the 1,500 K (Kelvin) of a candle flame up to the 30,000K of a crystal-clear, high-altitude, northern sky. The most relevant color temperatures that filmmakers and videomakers deal with are:

60-watt household bulb	2,800 K
Film studio lights	3,200 K
Photoflood lights	3,400 K
Sunset in Los Angeles	3,000 to 4,500 K
Noon summer sunlight	5,400 K
HMI	5,600 K
Blue sky light	10,000 K

The Quality of Light

Light controls every aspect of what we do. The care that we take with it will either enhance or detract from the perceived value of our final product. We are storytellers, and we tell our stories with light and sound. Take away the light and all you've got is a radio show. We paint with light. It gives depth and presence to a scene and creates mood. In order to paint with light you first need to see it in all of its nuance and spectrum.

The quality of light that is used in film production is developed and controlled by a small army of people who have spent the bulk of their lives refining methods and techniques for diffusing, re-directing and creating moods within the visual spectrum of illumination. There are hundreds of lighting systems from the enormous HMIs to the tiny Inky Dinks, incandescent, luminescent and strobe, each offering its own particular palette of luminance.

Modern video technology creates a recording environment that can shoot in a wide range of brightness values but has far less sensitivity than film. This doesn't mean that it records more colors or subtle shades than film, but rather that it is capable of recording in a much wider range of light intensities. Some video cameras are capable of shooting in situations where even the human eye is incapable of seeing. This gross latitude (that's "gross" as in encompassing) that is inherent in the digital video environment is one of the primary reasons that video always looks so flat and non-dimensional.

Painting with Light

Spend a little time browsing the paintings of the masters. (You don't have to leave home. Go to http://metalab.unc.deu./cjackson/index.html). Their whole world was tied up in the quality of light. Look at the way they handle shadow and form. By using light to define regions within the compositional framing of the shot we can create an enhanced perception of depth and dimension. Look at the shadows. Are they hard or soft, do they fall off rapidly or continue on? What angle are they coming from, what color is the light that caused them? The quality of light is often best described by the shadows it casts. The first step towards "seeing light" is in recognizing the importance of shadow.

Just getting the right balance of light to illuminate your scene is only the beginning. As previously mentioned, light is the essence of the scene. It creates the mood and atmosphere of the environment and helps to develop the character of the actor. A well-lit scene is often a combination of direct, diffused and bounced light sources.

A small direct light source directly above the camera (eye light) gives life to an actor's eyes while a direct intermediate spot directed at the back of an actor's head (hair light) helps to separate the actor from the background. A broad diffused or bounced light source behind the camera can keep light from direct sources like the sun from creating deep shadows around the eyes, and is, in itself, essentially non-directional.

One of the best exercises for lighting the human face is to put a couple of those realistic Halloween character masks on a couple of wig dummies and then practice with various lighting set-ups. For adding a really high-quality look to close-ups, try putting a strong, highly diffused light source above and slightly forward and to the side of the face. Take care to "cut" the light so that it doesn't hit the lens.

Since light falls off at a square of the distance, the soft contrast ratio that this set-up creates is quite attractive, especially when shot with a medium long lens. As foolish as this exercise may sound, by the time you've figured out how to get that Monica Lewinsky mask to look good you'll be ready for the big time.

PERSONAL STYLE

Lighting style is particular to the individual. Some DPs like to pull out every light they have access to and then fiddle with them for hours. I've worked with people like this and it is a costly and frustrating affair for everyone involved. I've also worked with DPs who can do amazing things with very few lights. One strong beam can be redirected and shaped into incredible environments by people who can actually "see light." I won't explain this but I will guarantee that you'll fully understand when you do get it.

Before learning to visualize light as volume, many people are amazed at how flat their images look when they finally see them projected. While our eyes view the set and actors in stereo, we are dealing with an essentially monocular system of recording and display. A quick and easy solution is to look at a scene through only one eye before you shoot it. A viewing filter will enable you to see contrast ratios and lighting balances more clearly.

VOLUME DYNAMICS EXERCISE

As an exercise in the subtle dynamics involved in lighting, rig a light a few feet above you as you sit in front of a mirror. Rig some method of focusing the light (aluminum foil barn doors) straight down so that it creates a pool of light a few feet wide on the floor, and then put a dark towel on the floor where the light hits so that there is little reflected light.

Turn off all other lights and sit under the beam while looking at your reflection in the mirror. Notice the harsh manner in which your face is illuminated. Now, cup your hands as if you were scooping up a handful of water and slowly bring them up under your face. Notice how the deep shadows under your nose and eyes are disappearing and the almost luminescent quality that this organically diffused, reflected source brings to your face.

Play with light. Experiment with it, bounce it, cut it, and figure out ways to diffuse it and learn how to make it do your bidding. Sit to the side of the beam and use white paper or cardboard to light your face using only reflected light. Notice how much softer and controllable the results are. As imperative as good lighting is to the conventional film production, it is even more important to video-to-film productions.

When you finally learn to "see light" you will truly become a cinematographer. Factors like resolution and platform will become less important to you than the quality of illumination. People who don't share your passion will muse at your predisposition to "tweak" your shots and "fiddle" with the lights. To them it will seem excessive. In the end, long after the inconvenience of your efforts is forgotten, there will be a recording of dimension and persona that will under-score everything you've done.

131

DIGITAL CRAFTSMANSHIP

The computer is passé; its days in the limelight are numbered. As the processor and those who personify it slip into obscurity we are starting to see a focus not on the process but on the results.

All the technology in the world won't make up for a lack in the basics of cinematic storytelling. As filmmakers we've really got only two tools at our disposal. Sight and sound. Since digital moviemaking involves substantial sacrifices, particularly in the visual dynamics of the finished product, we must seize every opportunity in the production process to enhance the perceived value of our final product.

Digital moviemaking parallels traditional filmmaking with the addition of understanding where and when accommodations for resolution, crew and production inertia must be taken into consideration. You've also got to have a firm grasp of both video and computer technology.

Combine this with a drastic reduction in the number of people among whom this expertise must be spread out and you'll realize that good digital film is potentially far more difficult to create. Not only do you have fewer people as a resource, but they each need to have a working knowledge of several aspects of conventional production methodology, and then be able to incorporate the vague nuance of technology and drastic budgetary limitations into the process.

Each aspect of the production process involves many years of evolution and refinement. It would be foolish to embark on a film project without having just a smattering of understanding with regard to the established methodology of conventional cinematic production. You won't just be wasting your own time but the time and resources of all those around you.

Low-budget film production generates a lot of stress and frustration. Never enough money, never enough time, never enough of anything but problems. It's all too easy to let it get to you, and you start becoming a tyrant. As soon as this happens you'll start losing momentum immediately and all your mealy-mouthed apologies the next day won't get you back on track. Always treat your cast and crew with respect. Take time to acknowledge their contributions and include them in decisions. Even if you know in your heart that you are the rightful heir to the Spielberg throne, be humble.

LINGO

Like all professions, filmmaking has its own language. These languages or "lingos" are essential building blocks that are all too often overlooked or misused. The contemporary film production unit is a complex organization of numerous specialized groups interacting with a common goal.

The director needs not only to understand what each group is capable of doing, but also how to communicate with that group so that his requests are understood. Of the many subset lingos involved in contemporary production, the four languages that the director must be fluent in are **Literary Language**, **Visual Language**, **Actors' Language** and **Production Language**. There are others but these are the basic ones that I feel are most relevant.

Literary Language

Literary language deals with character development, structure and timing. It is the vernacular of the screenplay. The essential foundation of any motion picture is described in this language in terms of empathy and structure.

Empathy is the essence of a good screenplay. Will the audience bond with and care about this character? All to often the inexperienced writer reverts to a series of hysterics or gratuitous confrontations to get the audience worked up, but this is just a cheap imitation of the true craft of evoking the most powerful of audience connections.

A truly empathetic character portrayal will cause a viewer to project his or her own personality into the character's situation and live the story vicariously through that character.

Structure is the style of architecture by which your script is constructed. There are formulas and rules of thumb, but the essence of any script's structure comes down to the central theme. In the simplest of terms, it is what the movie is about. Every element and character you can attach to it moves your story along. The plot is the sequence of events that move the characters along and create the ups and downs that identify a good story.

The way you put it all together and the voice you use to tell your tale make up the style. Great writers, great directors, great actors — all have a style that sets them apart from the others in their field. I heartily recommend Chris Vogler's excellent book, *The Writer's Journey,* for a far more through understanding of this most important element of moviemaking.

Visual Language

This is the language of the Cinematographer and Director. Back when I was a teenage camera assistant for the legendary Warren Miller, my limited uses of cinematic vocabulary specifically dealt with the question of loading film and where to place the camera. I never fully realized how integral it was to the greater whole until I took a class at USC back in 1986 with Ron Richards.

His approach essentially interconnects all of the classic Cinematic Languages and provides a very solid foundation from which to build a motion picture. Ron's most recent book, *A Director's Method for Film and Television*, and the two books by Steven D. Katz, *Shot by Shot* and *Cinematic Motion*, are great reference tools for the practical use of these languages.

The essential unit of measure is the "shot" where an action or performance is recorded until the director calls "Cut!" A group of related shots create a scene, and a group of scenes form an act, of which there are generally three in a conventional motion picture. The shot is visually described by the angle from which it is recorded, such as subjective, objective, or point-of-view.

Continuity is the flow of elements that pulls the audience along. Good continuity never lets up or offers the viewer a chance to disconnect with the story. Each new scene or location is established with a master shot, which tells the audience where they are and hopefully how they feel about it. After the situation is established, the camera moves in for a series of closer observations of the action or situations involved.

If the scene involves a dialogue between two people you might go in for a "two-shot" which is a medium framing that shows the proximity of the two characters. You might then move in for a "close-up" of a character's face, or an "over-the-shoulder" shot to further explain context and proximity.

Continuity also deals with the essential time base of the film, the color palettes, physical direction, lighting and tempo of the action, and eventually editing.

The lingo of editing is evolving daily as new production metaphors become accessible. Many of the terms from the mechanical age of film editing have made the transition into the digital age. Once a linen bag hung from a metal frame; thus the nonlinear environment still uses the term "bin" as a holding place for shots and sequences.

The selection, arrangement, and timing of the various shots into a continuous story is the essential goal of editing. The lingo involved spans the spectrum of narrative influence, timing, and esthetics.

Actors' Language

This language is as varied as the methods by which actors have learned their craft; many times you'll have actors from different schools on the same project. Developing a rapport and artistic bond with the individual actor is dependent on understanding what motivates that individual. Judith Weston seems to have a solid grasp of the metaphor, and her book, *Directing Actors*, is well regarded as a reference for contemporary dialogue between directors and actors.

To even brush lightly upon this topic is to incur the wrath of acolytes of the various schools of acting, and the industry in general, but here goes.

Almost all acting schools are derivations or combinations of the teachings of Lee Strasberg, Sanford Meisner, and Stella Adler, all members of Stanislavski's Group Theater in the 1930s. The essence of these teachings is to give the actors tools by which they can access their own emotions in the unconscious mind. Since the unconscious mind can't be controlled directly, students are involved in various exercises designed to evoke specific emotional correlates.

Even though the schools are all based on interpretations of the teachings of Stanislavski, their ideas are widely considered to be in conflict with each other. Stella Adler's interpretation is considered closest to the original Stanislavski; then Sanford Meisner; and then Lee Strasberg.

If I, a non-actor, were to attempt to briefly describe the basic themes of the various contemporary schools, it would be this:

Meisner is built upon **Immediate Experience**.
Strasberg is built upon **Sense Memory**.
Adler is built upon **Imagination**.
The **British** is built upon **Observation**.

The **Meisner** system seems to produce actors who pay better attention to their partners. Some of the basic Meisner exercises include the YES/NO and various repetition and back-and-forth exercises that tend to "bond" the actors together. *"Acting is living life truthfully under imaginary circumstances." "The emotional life of a scene is a river, and the words are the boats."*

The **Strasberg** system or "**the Method,**" tends to produce actors who are a bit more tightly wound. The system is based on SENSE MEMORY, which is the process of recalling all of the attributes of an object, and EMOTIONAL MEMORY, which is the process of recalling significant events and situations from an actor's past.

This produces the best actors for Blue Screen and affects performances, but often at the expense of an actor's mental health. Stella Adler once said about Lee that "*he would push people into spaces that they should not go without a licensed therapist present.*" Strasberg would often tell actors that they should get some therapy. Personally I feel the best improv exercises use sense memory. It catapults you into a sense of belief. PRIVACY IN PUBLIC. "*Visualize a real situation in your own life and do your lines within that frame of mind.*"

Stella Adler gives us the processing of action verbs and is based on imagination as being the best motivation for a good performance. The imagination is very powerful in the presence of a director who loves to tell stories. "*Get the verb of it, don't worry about the emotional thread.*"

The **British** approach to acting is an odd one. Not that it doesn't generate spectacular performances or consummate actors, but rather it is based on the actual achievement of acting. Rather than becoming the character emotionally or mentally, the British actor actually emulates a character by adopting all of the physical traits and characteristics.

Like I said, there's probably not a practitioner of any of these schools that would agree with my rather shoddy generalities, so do your own research or read Weston's book.

139

Production Language

This language essentially deals with the real-time business of making the connections, telling the story and getting the bills paid. This language starts with the budget and includes all the vagaries of finance and deal-making on an extremely sophisticated level.

When you're dealing with studio or distribution company executives, they most likely will be throwing around business school lingo. Don't fake it! What might sound like a really good deal in business school lingo might actually be the worst deal of your life. While there's no way to cram a six-year education into the development cycle of your movie, a great shortcut is to read the Friday copies of the *Wall Street Journal* and the *Hollywood Reporter*, front-to-back every week for a month.

IF IT AIN'T IN THE SCRIPT, IT AIN'T

Audiences go to movies to experience situations and sensations that will generate strong emotional reactions and insights. The structure, the characters and the conflict of the script must engage the audience and give them a revealing insight into the human spirit. A great script moves the audience along with a series of compelling visual elements (a picture is worth a thousand words) and uses the dialogue to glue the pictures together. This is true even if your movie never makes it any further than the Net. You must engage the audience!

If you're self-producing this is fine. The ability to make movies based on an innovative script is one of the primary motivations to the digital moviemaker. But if you're submitting your script to a studio, the script often causes problems. As I've already mentioned, the studios don't actually make movies anymore; they make deals.

As a result, the executives your script must engage are all lawyers or MBAs. A deeply revealing or emotionally insightful script is frightening to them. They're just not mentally equipped to deal with the subjective realities of deeply revealing interpersonal revelations.

Many of them try to adapt by finding ways to express subjective concepts quantifiably. There's always some new and tragically hip formula floating around Hollywood. It's like they all go to the same parties and hear the same neo-theological postulate, and next thing you know you're sitting in a pitch meeting listening to the Harvard Business School interpretation of the mise-en-scéne.

Instead of actually going out and developing promising actors they merely recycle the "safe bets" to the point where you'll see the same faces in four or five movies a year. Is it any wonder that the growing trend is to write bigger and bigger effects into the script or more spectacular obstacles to the character's goals? This formulaic, knee jerk manner of writing is merely an accommodation to the horrible lack of industry acumen at the studio level.

An independent script has far more latitude and should be wholly different from a studio script. There is no excuse for not developing the strong combination of revelation and sensation that creates the *dramatic center* of your script. The problem comes with the lack of subtlety that is available with digital productions because video simply doesn't have the dynamic range of film.

While motion picture film can capture the hundreds of thousands of subtle shifts in expression that echo pages of dialogue, the script destined to be shot in video must convey these thoughts more through speech and gesture. The greatest challenge for the digital scriptwriter is to create a boldness of action that treads the delicate balance between too much and not enough.

Unfortunately, the *dramatic center* is based on subtle revelations — and video is far from being a subtle medium. Instead of focusing on making the script or scene ''commercial,'' concentrate on evoking a series of emotional responses from the viewer. Creating an atmosphere in which the viewer can emotionally bond with the character is perhaps the hardest and most important objective in a video-for-film or video-for-Net script.

Don't keep the audience guessing about the character's persona. The more time it takes you to bond your audience to your main character's life and predicament, the more time they'll have to find fault with your film's technical shortcomings.

A 35mm feature can afford to spend time showing the audience around, getting them used to the environment and basically feeding them eye candy. You can't. Get down to business, get them involved, and do it quickly. If you haven't sucked the audience into your world in the first few minutes, chances are very good, unless you've got a real barnburner of a script, that you won't be able to reel 'em in at all.

It's not a bad idea to hold off on the title sequence until after they've had a chance to become vested in your principal characters. An even better solution is to suck in the ego a bit and put them all at the end. Titles are generally slow and plodding, a perfect time for the audience to criticize the quality of your image.

And once you're moving, don't let up, momentum is critical to the digital script. A 35mm film project can afford to back off the action here and there and allow the characters to "breathe" and have those small moments that offer up deeper insight into their hidden motivations. Not you. Stay on 'em and don't let up. If you keep the audience involved in the emotional roller coaster of the story they won't have time for anything else.

And when you're writing that witty repartee, don't forget to maintain a uniqueness in each character's voice. By keeping the lead's voice separate, you can keep it tied into the movie's *dramatic center,* with less reliance on the audience picking up on the more subtle indicators that would generally be used in a film script.

Where a film script would normally rely on dialogue primarily to express thoughts, and the actor's craft to express feeling, the digital script needs to incorporate subtle emotional indicators into the dialogue. Don't tell them what the character's feeling, but perhaps elaborate on the peripheral motivations involved.

Too often scripts become expositional in the third act, trying to tie up loose ends. This is the failure of establishing a solid base. Any basket weaver will tell you that a small mistake in the base will only get more notable as the basket progresses. With digital moviemaking this is particularly dangerous, because it lets your audience off the bus before the movie is over. Any glitches or shortcomings they missed earlier will leave with them.

SHOW ME THE MONEY!

A lot of people might disagree with my putting the budget under the craftsmanship chapter heading — but anyone who's been throughout the process will be glad to tell you that a good budget is a thing of beauty. It's not just numbers on paper, but rather the numerical expression of your vision.

A decent script with a funky budget has less chance of getting made than a mediocre script with an outstanding budget. Put a good script together with a great budget and you've got a true formula for success. Good budgets instill a sense of reliability and confidence in those silly enough to invest in your little venture.

With a red hot script and a realistic budget in hand you'll have the essential tools you need to go out and start raising money. Unfortunately, a good script is in many ways easier to generate than a good budget.

At the point at which you start to solicit money for your movie, you become a business, and as such need to start acting accordingly. Get yourself some legal representation. I know it sounds dreary and expensive, but there are numerous alternatives — such as Volunteer Lawyers for the Arts www.valny.org (east coast) www.calawyersforthearts.org (west coast) and the many guild and professional organizations that have legal counsel who sometimes help the occasional loose cannon.

Then there's the actual budget. Imagine that you've taken off your director's hat (budgeting for what you want) and put on your UPM hat (budgeting for what you need). At this stage the budget's primary job isn't necessarily to indicate where every penny is going, but rather to give your potential investors the reassurance that you actually have a firm grasp of the production process. There it is for them to see. Your understanding of the whole process, laid out in black and white. The bottom line is obviously very important, but how you arrived at that figure is perhaps even more important.

Since the budget is such an integral and necessary element of production, you might want to hire out this process if no one in your immediate production entourage has the aptitude. Don't feel bad. Many right-brained individuals have a hard time with the budgeting process. The important thing is to have someone who will keep you focused on it through the entire production process. Small extravagances at the beginning can snowball into painful overages by the time you hit editing. The result could be, and often is, a drastic reduction in the amount of resources left to print the video to film.

Perhaps the most common method of creating a budget is by templating. Essentially you beg, borrow or steal the most relevant current budget you can find and make the seemingly appropriate changes. The problem here is that movies are as different as people, and when you generalize a budget you are essentially "vanilla-izing" your entire project. Add to that, it's a lie — so you already don't have an auspicious start for a project that needs all the good karma it can muster.

When you finally get your budget worked out, give it to someone who's done this before just to make sure you haven't missed anything. Numbers are funny things. Commas sometimes look like periods and the next thing you know you're trying to explain why the video-to-film transfer budget is only $5.00. Little mistakes like that make you look careless and incompetent.

145

A far much safer and intelligent way to create a budget is to get some good budgeting software like Turbo Budget or Movie Magic Budgeting, and a copy of Michael Wiese's book *Film and Video Budgets*. It has a wide selection of samples from various production scenarios ranging from feature film productions all the way to "film school chutzpah." It also breaks down the cost per day of every job description in both standard and non-standard productions, as well as supplies you with a comprehensive list of industry standard budget codes.

DIGITAL DIRECTING

The process of storytelling is perhaps one of the oldest professions, yet the inherent dynamics that constitute a great storyteller are often misunderstood.

Moviemakers are predisposed to the one-way narrative, and as such need to maintain a strong visual presence in the mind's eye of the texture and pacing of the story elements. The director must also keep in mind the progression of various character arcs and how they interrelate, even though subsequent scenes in a picture might be shot months apart. This superhuman persistence of vision must often be maintained for a year or more, and is easily ravaged by drug or alcohol abuse.

In order to tell a rich and compelling story, directors need to have experienced life from both the valleys and the mountaintops. This comes with maturity. Look around at all of the truly great directors. They represent the full spectrum of the human condition and they generally have one thing in common — maturity. You, on the other hand, are a brash young Turk with fire in your loins.

Take a lot of deep breaths. The pressure and anxiety the directorial process creates can kill a career before it's had a chance to screw up on its own. Much of the pressure of directing comes from trying to fix compounded errors. You make a little mistake in casting or skimp on a location, and then whenever it comes up, instead of addressing it you aggravate the situation further by trying to work around it. These compounding phenomena have taken down many directors and their productions, large and small.

Always nip mistakes in the bud.

After years on the set I've come to recognize many of the basic traits of bad direction. I've occasionally caught myself falling into those patterns when talking to an actor. For me, being able to identify detrimental methods of communicating with actors has been a powerful, although inexact tool.

I recently took a seminar from Judith Weston that dealt with acting for directors. It was based on her highly recommended book, *Directing Actors*. Among the many inspirational and unusually relevant exercises that our class performed was an exercise that identified the trademarks of bad directors. Now, for the first time I actually had a quantifiable metaphor with which to measure my interaction with actors. With Judith's permission I've condensed it, paraphrased it, and here I am sharing it with you.

Trademarks of Bad Directors

- ### Result Freaks
  "Can you make it funnier? Can you take it down a notch?"

This causes the actor/director relationship to turn into a guessing game and forces the actor into a personal "bag of tricks."

• *Delivery Doctors*
"Don't say, I love you. Say I love you."

The director should be communicating the meaning of the line, not the inflection.

• *Process Servers*
"I think your character is very happy."

An actor who tries to have a feeling on demand looks like an actor.

• *Emotional Mappers*
"Okay, when you come through the door you're thinking that no one's home and then you hear something. You're disappointed because you wanted to be alone, but you're scared because you think it may be a burglar."

Psychologizing or mapping the emotional terrain of a character is the ultimate control device generally used by egotistic directors who don't trust their actors. Aside from being long-winded and tedious, this form of direction is counterproductive in an environment where time is at a premium. The result of this literal interpretation of the script will be a performance with no through-line.

• *Attitude Police*
" Show me how much you hate this guy."

Forcing actors into an attitude corner is the difference between doing something and showing something. Forced attitude creates posturing, which prevents actors from listening to each other. Nothing devalues a performance more than actors who aren't paying attention to each other.

• *Skitzo*
"He is happy but his heart is broken that she is leaving."

This pseudo-intellectualized method is intended to illustrate the complexity of the character. People are complex. They may say one thing while doing another, but they are not actually able to do two things at once. Divergent emotions cancel each other out, so the actor ends up faking them both.

• *Judgmental*
"He's an introverted geek," or "She's a slut."

Perhaps the most destructive device used for determining a character's make-up. Judgment forces the actor to telegraph the character to the audience. "I'm the good guy," or "I'm the villain." A director who uses this technique eliminates suspense by showing us the end of the movie when the character is introduced. The people in the audience should be the ones to make the judgments.

Good direction generates behavior in the actor. It is sensory rather than intellectual — and objective and specific, rather than subjective and general. It describes experience rather than drawing conclusions about experience.

The best directors actually do very little directing, but rather guide with questions. "What is important about this scene?" "What if the character just lost a family member?" "Do you feel like hitting him when he says that?" Howard Hawks used to say that he was merely giving the actors an attitude. "Once they've got an attitude, then it's up to them to do the lines."

There are, of course, as many styles of directing as there are directors.

One of my favorite analogies with regard to the director's role is from Robert Altman. I apologize in advance for any misquoting, as I was at a party when I heard him telling it, and I wasn't in any shape to take notes. Essentially he related making a movie to building a huge sandcastle.

In the beginning you're all excited about the concept of building a sand castle, so you sit around with some other people and design the thing and plan where and how to build it.

Everyone has a lot more opinions than you were expecting and the whole thing starts changing so much that by the end of the process you're almost ready to ditch the whole idea. Finally, the day comes that everyone planned and it turns out to be a really nice day, so you go to the beach and start building the thing. With all those people trying to help, it takes a lot longer to build than you thought it would.

It's getting hot, you've got sand in your shorts, it's looking totally different than what you had originally envisioned, and you can't wait for the whole thing to be over. Finally, just before sunset, you finish it. People like it or they don't. A large wave comes along and washes it away and you're ready to start planning the next one.

ACTORS AND THEIR NEEDS

Music videos, although not necessarily an appropriate metaphor for cinematic construction, deal with limited bandpass constantly. Many people whose videos play regularly on MTV and VH-1 also have robust cinematic careers. Madonna, Will Smith, Sting, and others are constantly dealing with the duality of film and video.

The almost unlimited latitude of film can generate thousands of gradations that constitute the range of expression, while most video only has several hundred shades of gray to work with. It is these subtle gestures and expressions that convey the hidden agendas and emotions that are so important to creating empathy and emotional connections.

Do your actors have more film or video experience?

One of the easiest and most effective ways to allow actors to adapt their style to your environment is to tape improvisations. The important point to remember is to light the set or area professionally where the improv is to take place. The simplest method would be to stretch a large diffusion panel above the area with a few crossed key lights.

Lighting and taping your improvisations gives everyone a test run.

You're killing several birds with one stone here. You're getting the actors comfortable with each other, and you're allowing them to metamorphose within the context of the production environment. Generally in very low-budget movies someone's girlfriend or wife is the designated make-up person. This generally entails little more than a smack with the powder puff and some light-colored lipstick for the guys, while the gals always seem to want to do their own.

By videotaping the improvs and rehearsals you not only give the actors a chance to make modifications and adjustments, but you also get an excellent opportunity to actually print a test. Take your best shot directly to your film printer of choice and have them make a minute or two-minute projection test.

Don't worry about sound and 3:2 pull-downs; just have them print a frame of video to a frame of film. Not only will you see just how much potential resolution and color-space your chosen video format has to offer, but you'll also be able to let your actors know how their make-up choices are transposing.

Imagine if you got all the way through production and postproduction, and finally up-converted and printed to film — only to find that all of your actors looked garish. Oh, they looked great on the video monitor, but up there on the screen . . . Don't be foolish. The two golden rules of digital video are:1) Don't stop shooting. 2) Don't stop testing.

There is a big difference between improvisation and rehearsal. Improv is an exercise in developing rapport between the actors and most importantly it creates a shorthand between the actor and the director. Once you start shooting you'll have so many things to keep track of, communicating with your actors will become a whole lot easier if you both have some previous common reference.

The goal of improv is to connect the subconscious of the character with the subconscious of the actor. A good improv should stress that there is no right or wrong approach. You simply can't do an improv incorrectly. Some may be better than others, but if you send your actors into an improv without obligations or judgments, you'll end up with a much happier kennel of puppies.

Rehearsal on the other hand deals with an actor's attempts to identify the emotional truth and core of the character. This process is best not practiced too much, because it can have the unfortunate effect of flattening out the performance. Your actors may feel that they've got the character nailed and merely regurgitate it back for you, rather than struggle with it and let it evolve before the lens.

In the end, you're going to want to look for performances that are truly different and compelling.

AUDIO

People get a little over half of their information about the world around them from their eyes. A classic study done at Yale revealed that people's influence is 55% visual (what we see), 38% vocal (the content of what we hear), and 7% verbal (how things are said).

Of course then you open the whole can of worms about the method of projection, the type of audience and which modality they are using to take it all in. Some people are more visual, or acoustic, or kinetic, in how they perceive things. But regardless of how you break it down, sound is one the most dependable generators of emotion the filmmaker has in the quiver.

Since all camcorders have built-in microphones, the first person to be eliminated from the low-budget production is all too often the soundperson. Ooops. The less experience you have in capturing high-quality images, the more imperative it is to have a competent soundperson and to create an environment conducive to recording a good audio signal.

First thing to take into consideration is the camera's built-in microphone. Do not use it! Even if you are a lone gunman, out there shooting away on your own, don't even think about it. The first rule in recording sound is to get as close to the source as you can without getting into the camera's frame.

If you're a one-man band and don't have a soundperson to hold the boom, get yourself the best "mini-shotgun" microphone you can afford. Attach it to your camera with a mount that has at least a little isolation to it; then get a "dead kitty" windscreen to cover the business end, and leave it there.

Any professional microphone is going to have an XLR plug, so get yourself an XLR adapter that can mount to your camera (www.beachtek.com). In addition to giving you a high-quality method of plugging in your high-quality microphone, a good adapter also gives you a way to manually adjust your sound. Like every other auto function on your camcorder, the automatic volume control should be super-glued in the off position.

Generally, the farther away the microphone is from the sound source, the more noise (ambient sound) it will pick up. The reason that you occasionally see boom mikes in pictures and television shows is not because these people are clumsy, but rather because they are so focused on getting the best sound possible that they often "push the frame" in an attempt to get the mike as close as possible.

The second rule in recording sound is to record your source as loudly as possible without over-modulating. You can always turn it down in post — but when you try to turn the volume up, you'll also be turning up any ambient noise that was recorded. One of the best ways to get good, dependable sound in a "lone gunman" environment is with lavaliere mics. These tiny mics can be hidden in clothes, behind ties and even in hair. Since they're close to the source they generally capture a fairly good signal. They can be hooked to a transmitter for wireless transmission to a receiver attached to the camera.

When you're behind the camera you've got enough to worry about without the added demands of acquiring a good audio signal. For this reason a soundperson is perhaps the most necessary addition to the small film crew.

The tiny meters and dials of the camcorder are not a viable alternative to accurate sound acquisition. This is doubly important if you're using a camera that doesn't allow for manual operation of the audio feed. It is for this reason that many, if not most small format video productions use an external DAT recorder. When using an external recorder, be sure to slate each shot with a good, crisp snap so that you can line everything up in post.

Most experienced soundpeople will tell you that once you set the level for a take, don't touch it until the take is over. The other thing they'll tell you is never leave a location without getting at least a minute of "room tone." This is simply a sample of the environment that the edi or can use to "glue" performances together at a later date.

Just as the environment shapes light, it also shapes sound. A set or location with flat, hard walls will bounce the sound around, giving the location a "hot" or "live" sound, while a location with soft furniture and objects on the wall will give a softer and less echoic (dead) sound.

One of the most serious drawbacks to tiny DV format is its inability to record a true SMPTE time code. I know the numbers on the camera's little LCD screen move like time code, but the unfortunate reality is that they're only a relative numeric reference that doesn't transpose. While this problem is endemic and affects nearly every aspect of postproduction, I'm putting it here under the audio heading because this is where it causes the bulk of its problems — and also where the majority of the solutions lie.

Many people use an electronic time coded slate (w/external time code generator) plugged directly into a DAT recorder. A snap of the slate will then give a good visual reference on the video image so the time code can be mated in post. It is very helpful if the soundperson runs a channel of audio back to the camera to use as reference. This is especially useful if you're going to transfer to D-Beta for your online edit.

Another popular practice is to record the time code from the slate's time code generator onto one of the audio channels of their DV camcorder. This gives them a permanently attached reference signal to which they can reference their DAT.

A time code slate is among the digital moviemaker's most essential tools. If for some reason you roll into another take without marking it, don't forget to add a tail slate at the end. Generally a small slate held upside down at the end of the scene should suffice. Make sure that your script supervisor makes note that the take was "tail-slated."

VISUAL EFFECTS

Feature-length cartoons, animations, science fiction and other effects-heavy, budget-limited projects need special consideration. Essentially, the playing field has changed so radically that today's PC has more crunching power than ILM did back when they made *Star Wars*.

By using rather inexpensive software on low-cost computers, you've quite literally got the potential to create anything you can dream up. Perhaps the most important thing to keep in mind when embarking on an effects-laden project is upward migration. Just because your project starts out on an iMac doesn't mean that it will end up on the same platform. This is such a simple, yet important concept that I am going to mount my trusty soap box for just a bit.

My wife and I have worked on numerous movies in the past dozen years where principal elements started as rough concepts on a laptop or desktop PC, and ended up in multi-million-dollar Inferno bays. The journey that an idea must take, especially a unique visual concept, is a perilous one. Every time you recut a gem, you lose some of the original beauty.

One of the first projects we worked on together was the original pre-visualization for *Jurassic Park*. It was an animated movie created in MacroMedia's Director software and rendered out in the Beta version of Apple's QuickTime (then called RoadKill). Needless to say, the project, despite its diminutive beginnings, went on to much higher resolutions.

That same scenario is replayed daily in the world of digital production, where cost-effective production technology initiates more ambitious projects. By creating a system in which elements of original thought and inspiration can easily be utilized by larger and more powerful production environments, you future-proof your intellectual property and increase your movie's potential.

GRAPHIC ESCALATION

Now I'm about as big a fan of Pinnacle's Commotion and Adobe's AfterEffects as you'll find anywhere. I was a beta-tester for both software packages back when they were far, far less stable; and I can probably attribute a substantial amount of my income over the years to projects and effects sequences that I've created using them. The biggest problem, however, has always been upward migration.

In numerous instances, projects started out with very limited budgets, so we'd use AfterEffects or Commotion in a desktop production environment. Usually the effects came out looking far better than the producers or the studio had imagined, so they'd go out and screen the rough-cuts for distributors and end up with much better distribution. Everyone won.

I remember when Adam Rifkin, Brad Wyman, and I were sitting around on my patio trying to figure out how we could physically make *Barb Wire* for two million dollars. Commotion, AfterEffects, and the rest of the desktop arsenal of applications played a big part in getting that movie off the ground.

We were well into physical production, and had more than a week's worth of shots in the can when the producers called from the infamous French Film Festival at Cannes. They'd seen a few rough-cut scenes and were so impressed that they started showing them around the festival. Nothing official, just "Hey, look at what these guys are doing with no budget."

They ended up raising many, many millions of dollars for that movie. A hot-shot music video director was brought in, more effects were added, and pretty soon the look started to shift from cinematic comic book (our original concept) to avant-cyber noir. *C'est la vie.* Many of the effects simply played as they had been created on the Mac, but since there was no real upward migration path, many others had to be totally redone from scratch on higher-end machines. A waste of time, energy, and money.

159

This lack of upward migration has long been a major factor in splintering the motion picture industry into the two distinct camps of high and low resolution. Anytime you've got a point of quantifiable separation, you're going to see technological effeteness rear its ugly head.

Ta-Da!

Combustion, from Discreet Logic runs equally well on Mac, or Windows machines, uses Adobe AfterEffects plug-ins and costs about the same (under $4,000) as comparable desktop applications. Essentially it's the fully endowed, younger brother of the multi-million-dollar Discreet Logic Inferno, which is the backbone of the high-end effects world. The cool thing is that everything you create in Combustion — masks, chroma-keys, rotoscoping and such — ports directly upward into the big machines.

As much as I hate to learn new software applications, I am learning this one. My wife — an Inferno artist with movies like *Godzilla*, *Armageddon*, *Mission Impossible II* and *Vertical Limit* under her belt — was an instant convert. Combustion is a "must have" for anyone considering a future in high-end video or film production. Does it replace AfterEffects or Commotion? Jury's still out. I only wish they'd come out with it years ago when I was a lot more tractable.

EDITING

In the late 1980s we started seeing the first wave of nonlinear editing systems. EditDroid, LightWave, Avid and others started attacking the status quo. For a hundred years, editors had been handling film with such unchanging mechanical tools as the Steenbeck, the

Moviola, and the Kem. Tons of equipment, some of it fifty years old or more, constantly churned out Hollywood's gross national product. Most, if not all, saw this digital invasion as an affront to the craft of editing.

The vast majority of the old school editors never did adapt and slowly slipped into retirement as a new generation of faster, more efficient editors took over the industry. In the end, it may be the director who tells the story, but it's the editor who translates it.

The old guard, with their lifetimes of "hands-on" craft experience, were being replaced in an instant by brash, young film students with several years of theory under their belts. The industry itself buckled under the blow as the tide of independent films began to swell.

The laws of film elitism require that every self-professed film lover proclaim the virtues of low-budget, independent cinema while bemoaning the dismal plight of the big-budget, studio blockbusters. Well, big budget or small, when it comes to editing, there is no other single element of the production process that so codifies the final product as being good or bad. Good editing can elevate mediocre directing and barely competent cinematography far beyond its humble birthright. Of course, it also works the other way around.

Sometimes it seems as though I've owned and used every major nonlinear edit system there ever was, including a prototype laserdisk-based EditDroid (1987), PC-based EMC2 (1989), 486 based-Lightworks (1991), Macintosh-based Avid Media Composer (off and on from 1990 to present), and the system that I've had in my house and have used on a daily basis since 1995, the Media100xr — pound for pound, pixel for pixel, my pick of the litter.

Occasionally I'll be working on a large project with traditional film editors who have just switched to nonlinear. In those instances the system of choice is generally one of the flavors of Avid because of the conventional film metaphor around which it is designed. The system you finally decide on should generate the highest possible resolution for your budget, be dependable, and be easy to use.

This section is not really about how to edit. You've either got the aptitude or you don't. You either know how you want to tell this story you've just spent a good deal of your life and resources on, or you're in big trouble. Technically, there's really nothing much anyone can really tell you that isn't covered better and more specifically in the instruction manual and tutorial of your chosen nonlinear system.

While the editing process is where your story comes together, in digital moviemaking it is also the stage of production where you stand the greatest chance of doing the most damage to your resolution. Image management is the name of the game here. The care you take in the editing process will be reflected upon the screen.

The simplest and perhaps best solution for maintaining resolution is to bump your selected DV "takes" up to D-Beta after shooting, and then sync in your DAT audio. Problem solved. This gives you a far more robust environment for editing as well as more channels of audio for mixing, and, of course, SMPTE time code. Now you can do your nonlinear offline edit using the D-Beta's time code. Once done, you can take the EDL (edit decision list) to a D-Beta online and have them edit your movie in a far more robust D-Beta format.

You'll end up with an image that easily has twice the resolution and color-space of an image that was transferred to your nonlinear edit system directly from DV and then recorded back out after editing for printing. This methodology increases the cost of your production a bit, but the gain in resolution and color-space will be its own reward. When you do finally get around to printing your movie to film, the D-Beta format will give you a far more stable and more widely accepted delivery mechanism, since most printers don't accept the mini-DV format.

The System

Get the biggest monitor you can. Better yet, get a couple of 'em. Like any good work environment, the surface area of your desktop has a lot to do with how easy it is to keep track of things. By the time you get into editing, the name of the game is data management. A sizable workspace goes a long way toward knowing where everything is.

Storage is one of those things you can't ever have enough of, especially if you plan on printing from your edit system's output. If you're editing at a really low compression ratio (2:1), the space that each frame takes up is going to be much greater than the space at higher ratios (50:1).

Don't count on storing your entire movie at a low compression ratio within your system unless you've got more than a hundred Gigabytes.

Get yourself a good orthopedic chair. You're going to be spending weeks in this thing. Make those weeks as pleasurable as possible.

The eleven-hour workday is fine for moving light stands and set pieces around, but no one can be creative in a continuous, eleven-hour-day work cycle. Physical exhaustion is much easier to recover from than mental exhaustion.

After working a hard, ten-hour day, you might be physically spent; but after a good night's sleep you'll usually be up and about, ready for another hard day. Exhaust yourself mentally, and you might

captured at 300Mbs

captured at 50Mbs

Notice the compression artifacts in the sky and around the hard edges of the giant killer scorpion.

need a week to recover. Digital production schedules should revolve around eight-hour days. Run three shifts if you have to crank out the work, but make sure that you give your people an opportunity to recover.

Rule of Thumb

Nonlinear systems all follow the basic rule of thumb: Digitize your selects, build bins for each scene, you'll never have enough storage, you'll never have enough time, and Coke and pizza are your best friends. Oh yeah, and once you've got it calibrated, don't touch the damn monitor!

The Process

Start the edit process with a highly compressed, "draft" quality image. Many people are quite content to complete the entire project in this ultra-low quality mode and then re-capture and re-edit the scenes in successive order. As each high-resolution scene is finished, it's recorded to the video master that you are taking to the printer, and then dumped to make room for the next scene.

As you re-digitize the video footage for your final edit, make sure that you run each take through the system's built-in, software wave-form monitor and vectorscope. It's a lot cheaper to color-balance here than at the printer.

The Work Environment

How you configure your edit system is up to you. The vast majority of people get a table and simply start piling equipment onto it. I've spent a good many years sitting among computers and production equipment, and, personally, the thrill is gone. I'm tired of the persistent whine of the drives and fans, and I'm tired of the techno-clutter. While, admittedly, my environmental preference falls way short of the norm, I offer them here for your consideration.

My own system is configured to meet my particular needs at what many people would consider the high end of desktop production. While it has evolved since this picture appeared in *RES* magazine's premiere issue, it represents an appropriate home production environment for anyone with a solid technological understanding, decent job flow and a dislike for structured corporate environments.

My basic home production environment is built around a dual G4 Media100xr system with twin 72Gb Megadrive RAIDs using a Wacom PL-300 touch-screen tablet as a control interface. By pumping the master edit feed into the component channel of my high-resolution, 1,000-line monitor, I can actually create and edit from my most comfy chair. So while all my machines whir and whine away ubiquitously in the next room, my friends and clients can hang out in a pleasant environment, rather than in a dimly lit industrial toy box (see page 200 in the Color Plates).

The atmosphere is much more conducive to conversation and collaboration; and since the image on the screen is big and bright, everyone can relax and see what's going on without hanging over my shoulder.

For more high-end work, I use Intelligent Paradigm's (www.IntelligentParadigm.com), VideoExplorer 2, HD I/O board in a rather burley dual processor G4. It squirts 4:4:4:4 video at 10/16 bits in either NTSC or PAL with simultaneous composite and RGB outputs. It also provides the best 4:2:2 interpolation and up-conversion to 4:4:4:4 that I've seen.

The VideoExplorer 2 is the cornerstone of the most powerful desktop video environment currently in use.

When you combine half a Tbyte of wickedly fast drives and the high-resolution version of Apple's Final Cut Pro (www.finalcutpro.com), you've got an honest-to-goodness, High-Definition desktop production workstation. When paired up with Discreet Logic's Combustion software, you're as close to a high-end graphics workstation as you're likely to get (unless, of course, you don't mind plunking down half a million dollars).

Today, just about every new desktop computer comes equipped with some sort of nonlinear system already installed. One of the cutest mini-systems is the Sony VAIO PCG-C1 picture book. A 400MHz screamer runs Windows with a built-in camera and a 1,024 x 480 screen, and the whole thing fits in a jacket pocket. We're not talking about resolution or size now, just a very convenient video sketchbook that you can use anywhere. A kid who works for me does amazing things with a Fire Wire and Adobe Premiere. It all comes down to what works for you and fits within your budget. There's always a way to work around resolution issues as long as you can identify them.

So, Where to Start?

There are certain aspects of conventional production methodology that don't really change because of innovation. One such thing is "Tone & Bars" in video and the counter in film.

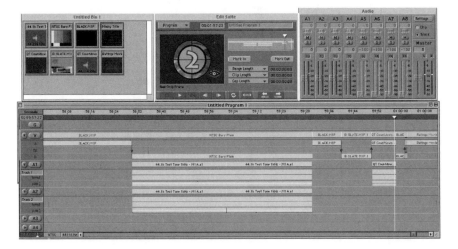

Shown here, the Media100 layout. Other applications will look slightly different, but the essential construction should appear similar.

Black at 00:58:00:00, then Tone & Bars from 00:58:30:00 to 00:59:30:00, then black to 00:59:40:00, then slate (includes the film's name, the production company and date. You'll later come back and add the running time) to 00:59:50:00 where you'll insert your countdown numbers and a beep at the top of each second from 10 to 2. At the end of the "2" you go black until 01:00:00:00 (one hour), where the program begins. Any creativity or liberties taken at this point will not only screw up every professional that comes in contact with your movie but will also make you look like a clueless dork.

Fade up from black....

SCORING YOUR EPIC

So you finally get to the end of your edit, and now it's time to add the score. This is how you subliminally tell the audience how you want them to feel about each scene and character. The thematic underscore creates mood and texture. A scene underscored with violins and trumpets can cause emotions to swell with majestic expressiveness, while a lone oboe can escort your audience into an almost cathartic empathy with a character.

In the standard Hollywood fare, all too often we see every gesture and nuance underscored with dramatic themes. The audience never gets a chance to breathe, or make up its own mind. On the other end of the scale is the small budget production that's forced to use "canned" music. Often the emotion and theme don't match, or the timing is off.

In these instances It's often better to lay down an audio reference track and edit the scene to the track. As blasphemous as this may sound, a good soundtrack has a pacing to it that's based on thousands of years of refinement. By editing your scene to that evolving thematic correlate, your scene takes on a tempo and pace that not only merges it with the musical underscore but also conforms it to an established tempo.

PRINTING TO FILM

This entire book is dedicated to squeezing the absolute optimum resolution, color-space and density out of your chosen video system. From the initial choice of camera through production and postproduction, everything you do affects the amount and quality of information that the film recorder must assemble.

Perhaps the most misunderstood and most mystifying aspect of video for film is the actual process that up-converts the video image and then prints it to film. Just as there are numerous flavors of compression, so are there a number of methods of up-converting the video image to a higher integer of data. This process is often called "up-resing" but there's no way to actually increase the amount of resolution you have after the production process is over.

You can tweak the colors, increase contrast, increase the number of pixels that represent the frame, but you can't increase the resolution. What you've got is what you've got. Live with it.

The most important consideration in the printing of your digital movie is your motivation. Why do you feel that you need to print your picture to film? Is it just to say that you've produced a "film," or are there other factors at work?

One of the most unfortunate aspects of many festivals is their continued insistence on a "film only" policy. This celluloid snobbery not only results in a drastic decrease in the inherent quality of the digital image but subjects the indie filmmaker to a $20,000 to $30,000 admission fee just for the transfer. By simply renting a GE Light Valve or other similar high-quality video projector, the indie festivals would emerge from their rut of pandering to the Hollywood ideal and truly become Meccas for the alternative forms of expression they claim to attain.

Only when the tools of production and distribution become freely accessible will the motion picture truly become an art form. Perhaps now that Hollywood is buying so heavily into digital projection, there will be a shift in the priorities of festivals as well.

But hey, (excuse me while I step down from my soap box) whatever your reasons, you've decided to print your epic to film. Let us kneel down at the altar of technogogary and pray for guidance.

I know that there is the odd post house that will print directly from DV format. But the only reason I can imagine for doing this is that you edited linearly within a DV native edit suite, never re-compressed and never used any other methodology whatsoever for storing or moving the signal around. Barring that unusual scenario, mastering back to a DV format, a format that has a significant 5:1 compression ratio, could be considered resolution suicide.

The vast majority of DV moviemakers use some form of nonlinear edit system. Most of those systems have the capability to sample in and record out in Y, R-Y, B-Y. Why would you ever want to re-compress your video at a whopping 5:1 ratio on the last leg of its very painful journey?

See, the problem starts when you sample your DV into your Media100 or Avid or D-Vision nonlinear edit system. If you use the Y/C (S-video) cable to transfer your video into the edit system, you are transposing the original format twice, because the two pieces of equipment use different compression schemes.

A lot of people think that if they master back to the format from which they originally digitized, things will magically be better. Not true. Compression causes a compounding degradation of the video image. In many instances it is far worse than the degradation caused by successive generations of analog copies.

If you've got a Fire Wire (IEEE 1394) or iLINK-equipped camera and an edit system that can accept and edit in the native compression scheme of that specific camera, you can forgo two very painful steps in the degradation of your image. The fact that you may be able to Fire Wire directly into your computer doesn't mean that the compressors that enable your nonlinear system are compatible or non-degratory. Sony DV is different from Panasonic DV, which differs from Canon DV; you've got various flavors of DV within the various manufacturers.

Don't get sucked into this "Digital is Forever" fallacy. Digital is a delicate mélange of ones and zeros. Like dropping a hand grenade in the middle of some marching battalion, compression drastically messes with formation. Every time you re-compress, you compound the deficit of the original compression. It's not simple math.

The most widely accepted method is to feed your finished edit out to D-Beta for transport to the printer. The data file (video frame) that arrives at the printer has been sampled, compressed, re-sampled and re-compressed, and then re-sampled and re-compressed and then re-sampled and up-converted. Using D-Beta the re-compression from the edit system's native format is only 2:1 instead of mini-DV's 5:1.

One important and almost always overlooked aspect of transposing from DV to D-Beta is that they are both compressed formats. Mini-DV at 5:1 must be re-sampled and re-compressed to D-Beta's 2:1 compression ratio. Not a really big deal if you're going to use your nonlinear system as an offline edit and then take your EDL (Edit Decision List) to an online, D-Beta edit facility for creating your final edit.

When in a position where I need to print to film from something that's come out of a nonlinear edit environment, the VideoExplorer 2 is the obvious choice. Regardless of the video's original flavor, the VE 2 interpolates the color-space and resolution using its hardware/software package to a 4:4:4:4, 16-bit image stream. The hot ticket is to then leave the whole thing on the disk, take your disk to your printer, and transfer the images in the greater color-space and resolution. By going to video, any video, I'd only compress and re-process the images one more time.

Before and After

Perhaps the most positive aspect of the video-to-film process is that the movie often takes on a saturation and richness that the digital version never had. Many people are amazed at the depth and texture that the transfer process creates and the almost subliminal enhancement of quality that the addition of grain adds. The flip side is a noticeable loss of sharpness, which can be catastrophic if you've already lost significant sharpness due to poor lenses or multiple compressions.

Color Correction

Color correction is critical to obtaining a good balance in your film transfer. Any variations in the hue, saturation or value of your color will only be intensified in the transfer process. Obviously, it's going to be a heck of a lot cheaper to do the color correction while you're still in the digital realm of the online environment. Use the highest quality broadcast monitor that you can get your hands on. Go out and rent a really good one just for color correction process if you don't already have one hooked to your edit system.

Once you've got a color-corrected master, it's time to head to the printer. Hopefully you've done a lot of tests and know the various shortcomings of all the choices available to you.

Transfer Options

Various video-to-film processes, in addition to creating different looks, also have different effects on your budget. Kinescope, the process of filming a monitor, is by far the least expensive method for transferring your movie. General prices run between $150 — $300 per minute for 35mm transfer, and half that for 16mm.

CRT Film Recorders, such as the Solitaire, are perhaps the most common method of transferring digital images to film. They basically work by breaking the video frame into separate red, green, and blue images. A very high-intensity black-and-white cathode ray tube then scribes each line of luminance individually for each of the three value frames in the image. When the red channel is being printed, a red filter actually swings into place as the cathode ray exposes each line individually.

For a 2,000-line resolution image, it makes 2,000 passes. Then the blue filter swings into place and the process is repeated, after which the green filter swings into place for the third process. After all three filters have been used, the film and the video both advance one frame and the process starts all over for the next digital image.

Back before printing computer images to film was a readily accessible service, I owned my own Solitaire film recorder and printed directly off the hard disk. Not only was this cruel and unusual punishment for friends, family, and neighbors (these devices are loud and obnoxious), but desktop jockeys all over the country were bugging me to do a test for them.

No matter how attractive the concept of owning your own film recorder may appear (you can usually buy a used one for the cost of a good transfer), don't do it! The time and money you waste on tweaking, film development hassles, and endless other woes will far overshadow and eliminate any potential savings.

Prices for a 35mm CRT print can range from $200 per minute all the way up to $1,200 per minute for the more sophisticated Electron Beam Recorder (EBR), depending on quantity of work and what the market will bear in your location. Figure on working out a deal for around $450 per minute for a long-form transfer.

Perhaps the best method of printing digital video to film is a direct digital transfer done with a laser recorder such as the ARRI-LASER. Hands down, no contest, end of story. The color palette is rich and full, the contrast is balanced and the grain looks right.

In the early days of digital production everybody was a technical engineer. The film printer is behind my right knee. Circa 1988.

Of the several facilities that are equipped to perform this technological wizardry, Tape House Digital Film (www.TapeHouseDigitalFilm.com) in New York City is widely considered to be one of the industry's leaders. Essentially they interpolate the incoming video frames to 2,000 lines of resolution, then print these digitally blown-up frames directly to film using a laser beam. A standard long-form transfer generally runs in the neighborhood of $650 per minute.

While a bit more pricey than a conventional CRT or EBR process, the laser printer creates an esthetically pleasing frame of film. For those projects that do have the finishing money for a high-end transfer, this is the way to go.

The decision about which method to use must obviously be weighed against the potential recoupment of your movie. Is it quite simply good enough to warrant a further investment of $50,000 for a full-blown, 35mm, digital print, or would a nice $6,000 Kinescope, 16mm print serve your purposes just as well?

Your success or failure in this area will be almost entirely dependent on the quality of the final resolution that you end up with and how methodically you researched all of your available options. If you're making a movie in Kansas, and the only film printer for a thousand miles is in Kansas City, get yourself on a bus and go either east to New York City or west to Los Angeles. Hang out and investigate every option you have.

Talk to other filmmakers, scout the online resources. Any shortcuts or wrong turns taken here will haunt you every time you project your movie.

LOW REZ

"Empty pockets never held anyone back. Only empty hearts and empty heads." — Dr. Norman Vincent Peale

You've made up your mind to shoot your movie in mini-DV and that's all there is to it. Okay, let's work with it. There are essentially so many variations that it would be impossible to cover them all, so let's pick the worst-case scenario and then you can make adjustments with regard to your own production.

Situation: You've got a barn-burner of a script and a new credit card with a $10,000 limit. That's it.

Figure out a production time line and then stick to it. One of the most important elements of success is to have a set of specific goals that you can articulate. Now, everyone that joins your little crew knows where they're going and when they need to be there. Goals give focus, and deadlines give the whole production a pace. In a large production this is a natural byproduct of the budget and scheduling. Smaller productions often wither away from tomorrow-itis. Create an intelligent schedule and then stick to it — because a goal without a deadline is only a wish.

Get a *Recycler* magazine from the closest metropolitan city and do the bulk of your shopping from it. You can also check out this book's online persona at (www.PixelMonger.com) for deals on used equipment and production packages. You should be able to pick up a good used, Fire Wire equipped mini-DV camcorder for $500. The important thing here is to shoot everything in 16 x 9 aspect ratio, so you're going to look for a camera that actually uses a 16 x 9 imaging chip. Since your choices here are severely limited, your next best option would be to get a camera that stretches the conventional 4 x 3 (Panasonic, Canon) image rather than one that crops the top and bottom of the 4 x 3 (JVC, Sony). **Total: $500**

For a simple option you could check out one of the several reputable used equipment dealers like B+H Photo in New York City (www.bhphotovideo.com). They are more expensive than buying out of the *Recycler* but then you've got a camera that is backed by a substantial and reputable company.

Next look around for a used DV iMAC or, better yet, a used G3 or G4 with at least 256Mb of RAM and the largest monitor you can find. The Mac should cost under $600 and hopefully comes with Apple's very hip editing software package, Final Cut or Adobe Premiere 5.0 or higher. If you can score a copy of Final Cut Pro do it.

Since you're going to need to stay in the 16 x 9 aspect ratio without re-processing your image, consider buying the DV ToolKit from ProMax (www.promax.com) for $200. This software plug-in allows you to edit in Final Cut in native 16 x 9 aspect without further degradation to the signal's integrity. **Total: $800**

Fire Wire is going to give you about 4-1/2 minutes of audio and video per Gigabyte, so figure on picking up around 80Gb of Fire Wire drives so you'll have room to move around. Sometimes you can find really good deals on drives, but you never know where they've been, so it's not a bad idea to bite the bullet and get some new ones. ProMax sells a really good 37Gb for around $400 each (get two), and they have the most knowledgeable sales staff in the industry. **Total: $800**

Pick up the best-used, mini-shotgun microphone you can find for around **$100** and you've just slammed together your entire digital production environment for a tad over $2,000.

The bad news is that since this system is built around the 4:1:1 mini-DV format, you're starting out at 5:1 compression ratio with greatly reduced color-space. The good news is that it won't get any worse. The Fire Wire accommodates the DV's 3.6Mb second data rate with room to spare and the DV-friendly Final Cut edit software is transparent to the final image.

Equipment

Foam core reflectors from the art store and a white Army surplus parachute are the two most important elements of your outdoor shooting package. For interior shots consider bouncing sunlight into the room from reflectors (aluminum foil-covered foam core) located outside in direct sunlight. Once you start with lights, you've gotten into an area that costs money.

Many rental houses carry inexpensive lighting kits, like the Lowel DP light kit, that are quite versatile. Just remember that you're trying to achieve a film look so you're using the ND filters, right? **Total: $100 per week rental**

Almost as important as the lights themselves are the tools to bounce, diffuse and cut the actual beams. Again, foam core with reflective surfaces as well as black. A good hardware store will have spring clamps that look somewhat like large clothespins. Get a dozen of these as well as a few rolls of double-sided foam tape and several rolls of duct tape. (Since you're a filmmaker, you should always call it grip tape once you're out of the hardware store.) Total: $100

Production

Drive your production or it will drive you. Hopefully you've gathered a few friends around to help with the actual shoot, and you've even got a few actors from the local school or workshop to work for free. If they are professional actors, you've made a deal to pay them a deferred SAG salary if the film gets distribution. The important thing to work on here is not so much the technical aspects of the production but rather the social skills involved in keeping everyone happy and focused. More than any other aspect of no-budget production, teamwork and a congenial environment will lead to a successful shoot. **Tape stock: $100. Food: $100. Slush: $100.**

Often overlooked in micro-productions is the obligatory "wrap" party. I know that you're short on funds but there is simply no better way to say thank you to all the people who put up with your sniveling insecurities and unreasonable demands. Beer, wine, pizza, and a bottle of good tequila. **Total: $250**

Editing Software

Apple's Final Cut Pro works equally well with PAL or NTSC and is a little easier to use than Adobe Premier.

Editing

Since DV needs only about 18Gb for 90 minutes and you've got room to spare, you can forget offline editing altogether. Just sit your butt down and get it done. Either you've got the ability or you'd better know someone who does.

One of the seemingly endless bits that you must track is the length of the actual reel of film. Unless you want the audience to know when the projectionist changes a reel, you'll need to adopt a well worn strategy.

Divide your movie into 20-minute segments (19 minutes if you're editing in PAL) so that at the end of your first reel you have a scene cut. This will keep the unavoidable differences between the various reels from becoming apparent. Even though the reels are all developed by the same lab, they most likely won't be developed in order. Chemicals in the development process are constantly changing and often produce noticeably different colors and densities between head and tail.

Data Transfer

The least expensive way to transfer your data is to simply clone the segments back out to your camera via Fire Wire. Keep in mind that the duration of a camera is more limited than tape decks. Unless your DV camcorder is true 16 x 9 native, which it probably won't be, there could be significant degradation to the image.

A better method is to clone your movie to another digital format such as DigiBeta or D1, or get yourself a Sony DSR-30 DV record

DIGITAL MOVIEMAKING / Billups

deck ($3,000 new). This deck records in 16 x 9 aspect ratio and accepts the larger and longer 3-hour DV tapes. Since it is an IEEE 1394 native system, there is essentially no distortion of your delicate signal. You might luck out and find a used one for $900 or less, but plan on doing a rather aggressive search. **Total: $900**

Printing to Film

The EBR (Electron Beam Recorder) is out. Maybe even the $6,000 to $12,000 for a decent Kinescope is out. I guess the first order of business is to evaluate the reason behind your need for a film transfer in the first place. Is it for submission at a film festival or a screening at a theater? Does it need to be 35mm or will 16mm suffice? How many copies are you going to need? Once again, there are so many variations that it would be impossible to cover them all, so let's stay with this worst case scenario that you only want a single 16mm print for that special film festival.

Here you are with your project already edited and scored. Oh yeah, throw in $200 for a canned soundtrack. You've been meticulously careful with your data stream and it is essentially in pristine condition as it sits on the computer's disk. **Add: $200**

Kinescope, the process of filming a monitor, is by far the least expensive method for transferring your movie. Companies like Ringer Video in Burbank use a high-quality monitor and a special camera that runs at 23.976 fps to achieve a flicker-free transfer. They generally charge around $50 for a one-minute, 16mm test and $80 per minute for the actual transfer. Go for the test. This will give you a good reference for what you can expect from your inherent resolution. **Total: $50**

Hopefully there aren't any unpleasant surprises and your meticulously cared-for image still looks good when projected. Heck, if you can afford it, have them do the whole thing; otherwise...

CAMERA

There is quite a selection of 16mm motion picture cameras out there and if you don't already have a personal favorite, you might want to consider renting an Arri-S, 16mm MOS (without sound) camera from someone like Alan Gordon Enterprises for a week. You'll need it long enough to do a test, get it developed and then check out your footage. **Total: $225**

Film Stock Selection

The inherent sensitivity of a film to light is expressed in terms of its ASA (American Standards Association). A *fast* film stock needs less light to register an image than a *slow* stock does. Rule of thumb is that a film stock rated ASA 50 or less is considered slow, while an ASA of 200 or above would be considered fast. The ASA 50 film would need twice the amount of light or an increase of two stops on the lens aperture to achieve the same exposure as the ASA 200 film stock.

Of course you've got to make your own decisions, but I like the grain and color-space of the 16mm, Kodak 7277, 320 ASA, Tungsten negative film stock for this process. Keep in mind that this is a twin-sprocket stock, which will give you far less gate weave but a slightly smaller image area than the single-sprocket variety. Since you're eventually going to want a 1.85:1 protection mask, the slight side cropping from 16 x 9 to the narrower 1.85:1 won't be a big deal.

185

A 1,200 foot reel will cost you in the neighborhood of $400. Normally I'd recommend going to a company that sells short ends for the ultimate in economy, but that would entail a substantial amount of splicing and editing, something you don't want to get involved in. By recording your movie on three 1,200 foot reels you've got a cross-projection package that just about any festival can deal with. **Total: $1,200**

Controlling Contrast

One of the biggest problems inherent in the Kinescope process is contrast. Professional labs that do this have made accommodations to their CRT. They know how different films handle and have gamma settings that correlate to the nuance of each stock. You, on the other hand, must use another method to reduce the contrast/gamma.

The simplest solution is to add a low-contrast filter, but it has a tendency to reduce the color saturation in this environment. TEST!

There are several devices such as the Arriflex VariCon, that mount to the front of the lens and shine a low-level light into the front element. This is a great tool for conventional studio and location work, because it allows you to actually see the amount of contrast that you're controlling. The biggest drawback, using a VariCon type of device in Kinescope, is that the light has a tendency to reflect off of the front surface of the monitor, giving you a hot spot in the center of your picture. Besides, this is way out of your budget.

Perhaps the most widely used method of lowering the gamma (also reducing grain in many stocks) is to underdevelop in processing.

This is called "pulling" and any good lab can do this, although they do charge a bit more. Essentially, the film is overexposed when you shoot, generally by a stop, so in processing you ask them to "pull a stop."

If you're using an ASA 100 film you'd meter it for 50 ASA. I personally like the results of pulling. It adds an inherent richness to the scene — and you're going to need all the richness you can get. TEST!

Another method is to *pre-flash* the film. To do this, you simply run the film through the camera in a dimly lit room. What it ends up doing is increasing the exposure of the shadows while not affecting the brighter parts of the shot.

Let's say that you've got a 12 x 12-foot room. You'd put a white card on the wall and then place the camera about 9 feet from the card, making sure that the card's image fills the view. Then crank the focus in as close to the lens as it will go and stop down to $f8$. You want to use a combined light source that is about 10-candle power with a slightly warm color temperature. Those small Christmas lights work quite well.

Mount one of these tiny lights on either side of the camera about two feet out from either side of the camera body. Make sure the lights are well behind the lens. This is based on a 180 shutter and an ASA of 200. Make accommodations for shutter angle based on the fact that light falls off at a square of the distance. A narrower shutter needs more light or wider aperture. TEST!

The Shoot

Liquid Plasma Displays (LPD) are similar to the Liquid Crystal Displays (LCD) on laptop computers except they are much larger and far brighter. Like LCDs they don't flicker when filmed, so you don't need to make accommodations for frame rate. They are, however, expensive. If you don't personally know someone who actually owns one of these marvels of modern technology, go to a store that sells them and plead with a manager to let you run your video through the system while you record it with a film camera. If whining and groveling doesn't work, offer money. A couple crisp Benjamin Franklins should do the trick quite nicely and assure you of an uninterrupted, after-hours Kine session. **Total: $200**

Rig a 1.85:1 mask onto the front of the camera. Turn off all lights, or, better yet, surround the path between the LP display and the camera with duvetyn or black cloth. Run an 85% gray signal through the monitor and use a light meter to get the appropriate setting.

Test

Hopefully you've made a deal that allows you to run a test so you merely bracket the exposure using successively larger and smaller apertures. You need to keep meticulous notes as to which f stop you are using. The best thing to do would be to cut several seconds of various scenes with dissimilar lighting together and then superimpose the successive f stop numbers over the various clip combinations. When the clips are played through the monitor, you simply set the f stop on the lens to match the f stop that is superimposed on the shots, and then there won't be any confusion when you're sitting in a dark screening room trying to make your critical decisions.

Developing

Generally a good lab like PhotoChem in Burbank will work with you quite a bit on the processing. They've been around a long time, and realize that when they help out a little guy, they're often creating a customer for life.

Back in the '70s, when I was scavenging short ends to do little 35mm projects, I became quite familiar with their night shift. The few invoices that they did give me were very reasonable. Generally, they'll even do your tests and throw in screening for under $50 a pop. Figuring that you're going to process 3,600 feet, you'll be able to get a deal (now don't quote me on this) for around $600 for your negatives and around $1,200 for your print. Depending on how well you configured your audio tracks, they should be able to lay your sound down with a minimum of additional cost. **Total: $1,800**

FESTIVAL TIME

So now you've got your print and there's a festival that's got you in their cross-hairs. Now is the time to really turn up the effort, and don't be timid about blatant self-promotion. Make a concerted effort and maximize every opportunity to establish or increase your Internet presence. Remember that a strong Internet buzz is both self-propagating and compounding.

Always remember that "Advertising is what you say about yourself. Public Relations is what others say about you." An ounce of PR is worth a pound of advertising — and the nice thing about PR is that it's practically free. The popular misconception is that PR means Press Release. As annoying as these terse missives were in the early days of faxes and desktop publishing, the Internet has allowed them to breed like mosquitoes in the pixelated pool of online interconnectedness. You *must* create a unique voice that will break through the media clutter and enhance the perceived value of your project.

Good Public Relations are as inseparable from public opinion as the grassy knoll. It should always be based on your project's strongest points, and echo the timbre and voice of the film. Keep driving these same points over and over regardless of how repetitive you may feel they are. Actively seek out interviews about the project and line up interviews for your actors as well. Send the best VHS dubs you can generate to people who write articles for film and entertainment magazines. A little personal attention from you can generate enormous returns in PR.

Unless you really hit one out of the ballpark, PR is going to give you the highest return on your investment. You've got duplication and shipping charges for thirty dubs with really nice labels. **Total: $300**

You've now got a little over $2,000 left from your original $10,000. Consider this your Transportation, Housing, and Schmooze fund. Whither goest thy film, so too shall ye go. And when you get there, don't hesitate to buy the next round. *Always* drink less than half of what you're pouring down potential patrons, and *never* stop schmoozing your ass off.

Don't get involved in relationships that aren't business-related. A lot of deals have been lost because a newbie filmmaker was busy hustling up company for some late night tryst rather than sniffing out business and promoting the film. Oh, and have fun. People see you having fun, they'll figure that you're a fun guy or gal and that you've made a really fun movie. And don't forget to put me on your guest list.

"The first 90 percent of a project takes 90 percent of the time. The last 10 percent takes the other 90 percent."
— *Peter Marx*

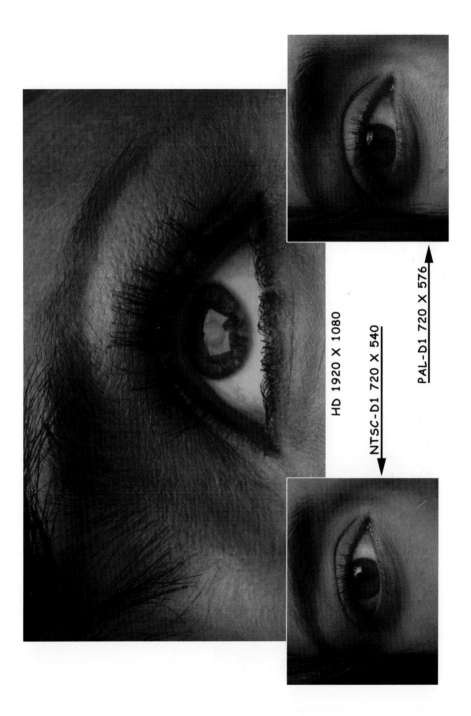

HD 1920 X 1080

NTSC-D1 720 X 540

PAL-D1 720 X 576

DIGITAL UP-CONVERSION
ALL IMAGES HAVE BEEN COLOR TIMED AND DENSITY CORRECTED.

35MM MOTION PICTURE FILM

SONY HD700 HI DEFINITION

SONY DIGITAL BETACAM

PANASONIC DVC PRO 50

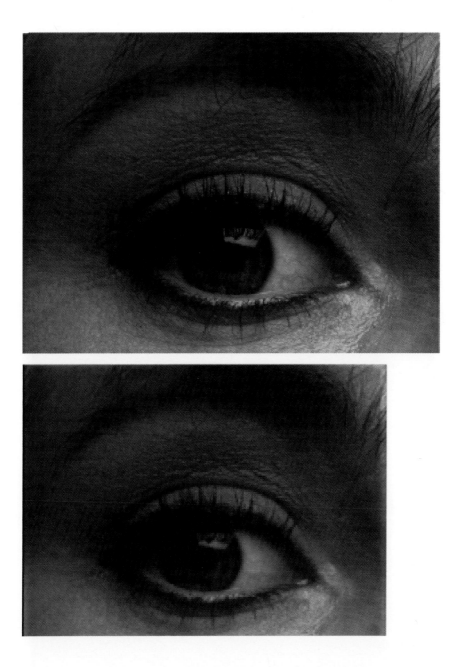

The same image taken directly off of the CCD (above) and off of the tape (below).

This is how every shot should begin. Then slate, then sound, then action.

The circle is a focus chart, and will help you determine how sharp your lens really is. The gray scale chip chart can be used in conjunction with a waveform monitor to adjust the light response (video levels and gamma). When you view the chart on video playback, you should be able to make out all five chips. If the lightest one blends in to the page, then your gamma is set too high. If the black and the dark gray merge together, then you're crushing your blacks and need to adjust the pedestal.

We are finally entering the age of ubiquitous technology.

BYTE-SIZED CHUNKS

As much as Hollywood would like us all to believe that the cinema screen is the moviemakers pinnacle of success, it is access, more than size or resolution, that will drive us into the future.

The Internet is not, as so many put it, "a digital gold rush," but rather the purest form of free enterprise in the entire history of mankind. Anyone of above-room-temperature IQ, who doesn't at least give mind service to some harebrained, entrepreneurial scheme, is missing out on this lifetime's golden opportunity. Just about any topic, product or service has its niche in this bitstream of humanity. And you, well you've got one of its hottest commodities — content.

You've made your movie, invested time and resources far beyond your original intention, and now you're pondering the myriad choices of distribution scenarios. Maybe you're planning on releasing your mini-block-buster through one of the many independent film sites on the Internet.

Ahh, that's the ticket. Just sit back and let them generate clamoring throngs of ardent fans. After all, movie sites are one of the fastest- growing venues on the Internet. Generally all you need to do is send them a DV copy of your movie and they'll prep, compress, and post it for you.

While some sites deal mainly with a certain style or genre, others offer a wide spectrum of content — from Flash cartoons and animations to mini-theatrical releases. Of the hundred or so sites dedicated to online cinema, Atom Films, Short Buzz, Always Independent Films, and Honk Worm are widely considered to be leaders in their categories.

Atom Films (www.AtomFilms.com) is one of the Internet's premiere innovators, and offers a broad assortment of titles in a wide
selection of bandwidths and players. Its founder, Mika Salmi, is
well known for his unique and well-articulated view of the industry.
So when I ask him what he looks for in submissions from new
sources, he says, "Quality, always! And projects that take advantage of the new mediums, such as the interactive nature of the
Internet or the portable, on-demand nature of handheld devices.

"Right now," he says, "everyone is focused on short-form and low-
bandwidth-friendly technologies, both of which are extremely
important today; but there's a place for all approaches. Live action
films are quickly catching up to "made for the Web" animation
technologies in popularity. All genres and lengths will eventually
work in these new platforms just as they do in the rest of the media
world. That doesn't mean that there won't be whole new kinds of
entertainment that take advantage of the new distribution platforms.
Those will exist, too.

"The other thing," he adds, "is that the Internet offers unique
opportunities to build communities of artists, entertainment enthusi-
asts, and consumers. This means that artists have direct access to
their audience, and both artists and consumers can directly determine what entertainment they want to make and see. In the future,
neither the artist nor the consumer will need to depend on a movie
studio to accomplish their goals or make available the kind of entertainment they want. This is truly revolutionary."

Gary Zeidenstein of Always Independent Films (www.alwaysi.com)
thinks that the leaders in streaming media will soon evolve into a
unique variation of a cable channel. "Right now we have a lot of

splintering going on in media distribution. Content plays different-ly depending on which environment you are plugged into and the bandwidth of that content stream."

"Convergence is constantly pulling audiences in different directions, but as soon as the television and the computer have finished merging into their final form, it will be hard to tell the dot-coms from the con-ventional broadcasters. The true difference will undoubtedly be the inherent quality of the content. There is a broad palette of opportunities for moviemakers who can adapt to these changing venues."

Not all dot-com honchos are solely vested in the Internet's growing parade of pixels. Honk Worm's (www.HonkWorm.com) President of Cross Media has a shelf full of the top accolades in broadcasting, including numerous Emmys, Peabody Awards and Golden Globes. Having overseen the development of such shows as "The X-Files," "In Living Color" and "The Simpsons" for Fox Television, and then "Ally McBeal," "Chicago Hope" and "The Practice" for David E. Kelley Productions, Jeffrey Kramer personifies the high-caliber profile of the Internet's big guns.

I asked Jeffrey what there was about this new environment that could possibly lure him away from one of the more successful careers in conventional broadcasting. "Streaming allows an unbe-lievable democratization," he replies. "In traditional media and broadcast, we tapped into talent pools in Los Angeles and New York and maybe Chicago. With Honk Worm, and the other online venues, creators can generate content from Martha's Vineyard or Pocatello, Idaho, or the bayou in Louisiana. We provide a platform for talents that would never have been found using the traditional approach."

When asked what he looks for in submissions, Kramer replies simply, "The quality of an idea. Traditional entertainment has a more laid-back style to it. You're physically sitting back to watch an hour of "The Practice," or a half-hour of "Seinfeld." With online entertainment you're generally sitting there leaning into your monitor. It has a lot more urgency to it and is much more interactive. You generally can't get away with as many characters, because you simply don't have the time. Maybe you're just dealing with an emotion, an ethic, a moral, a feeling, or a point of view. In some ways, it's like Harry Cohn's ass. If it wiggles in the seat, the story isn't good."

Another Hollywood veteran who's given up the rat race for the online lifestyle is Robert Algeri, who, along with his brother Dion, founded Short Buzz (www.Shortbuzz.com). "This technology is going to end the reign of the Hollywood power-brokers," Robert says with a mischievous gleam in his eye. "Finally, finding an audience for your film is easy. Before the Internet, if a film got past the gatekeepers at a film festival, maybe 50 people would see it. On the Internet it's likely that it will be seen by tens of thousands of people." He adds, "We're really just giving filmmakers the tools to promote themselves."

When I ask about how they feel about the state of technology that defines the Internet distribution mechanism, brother Dion replies energetically, "Frankly, it sucks! A grainy, postage-stamp sized RealPlayer screen really can't compete with television, so we don't try to compete with TV."

According to Dion, the success of the Internet is that it allows sites like their Shortbuzz to offer content that is fundamentally different from other entertainment venues. "We had a film on our site called 'Diet Pink Lemonade.' It was about thirty seconds long and profoundly stupid. It's about a man who destroys a little girl's lemonade stand because she doesn't offer diet drinks. It would never make it on TV, yet it's one of the most popular films we've had on Shortbuzz. Short, funny, unique and unavailable anywhere else."

But let's say that your movie has a special nuance that these guys just don't get. You've sent clips to twenty or thirty of the main movie Web sites but nobody shares your vision. Perhaps you posted some clips at DigitalFridge (www.digitalfridge.com) or your trailer's been running at TrailerVision (www.trailervision.com) for a couple of weeks and still the phone hasn't rung.

As marvelous as your movie may seem to you, and even though your mother thinks it should be submitted for Academy consideration, you've got a daunting task to generate an audience. Don't get me wrong; your audience is out there. You'd be hard pressed to create any-thing of any value that didn't appeal to *some* sort of market segment. The trick is to connect with the right market segments (audience), and connect in the right way.

THE FINAL INJUSTICE

The technology that drives Internet content more than any other is compression. All your hard work, the effort you put into salvaging and protecting your delicate signal, is now about to be crushed like an empty soda can. In fact, if we were to extend that metaphor, the compression that you are faced with would equate to reducing the soda can to where it would fit nicely between these parentheses ( ).

Hopefully this isn't the final stage of your production, but rather an integral step in the promotion and greater distribution of your epic flick. Let's say that you've been careful about the acquisition and management of your video signal, and you've ended up with a rather respectable 601/4:2:2 signal with a clean 44 kHz stereo soundtrack.

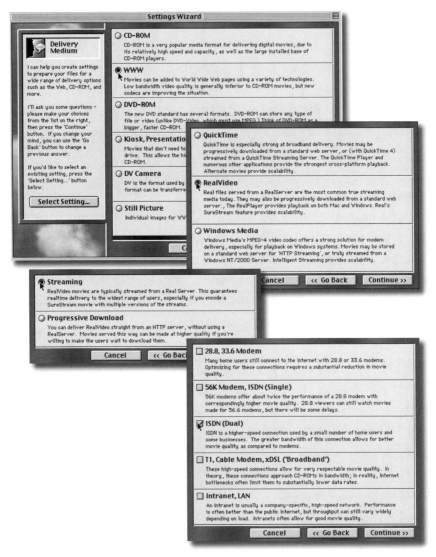

MediaCleaner's well-designed interface painlessly walks you through an otherwise daunting task.

Let's also assume that you've gotten yourself some sophisticated compression software like MediaCleaner (www.terrin.com) and you're now faced with major compression choices. As this book goes to press, Sorenson (www.s-vision.com) is the current choice of compression algorithms, and MediaCleaner is the leading software processing application. Virtually every major desktop software program (Adobe Premiere and AfterEffects, Avid, Media100, Edit DV, and Final Cut Pro) is now including a basic copy of MediaCleanerEZ with its application.

One of the many cool things about MediaCleaner is that it conducts a unique interview that takes you through the process of compression, allowing you to compile a series of intelligent choices based on the factors that are relevant to your project and market. MediaCleaner's manual alone is perhaps the singular, definitive resource for dynamic media compression. (It is one of the few software manuals that is so well written and laid out that it warrants a cover-to-cover reading.)

The final decisions with regard to size and data rates should be based on the collective bandwidth of your prospective market. Do you compress for the relatively limited, industry-average modem speed, or DSL speeds? Do you make your movie into a downloadable QuickTime, or do you utilize streaming technology so it can be viewed in quasi-real time on the Web? All these questions and more are addressed as you click your way through MediaCleaner's unusually friendly Wizzard interface. For those with a bit more confidence in their technical acumen, there's the Advanced Settings panel that allows you to configure your own compression battle plan.

207

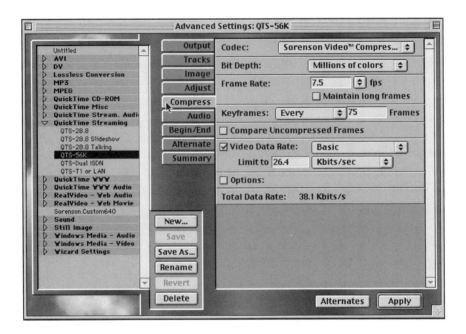

For those who love to tweak, Advanced Settings offer seemingly endless options.

SIMPLE MATH

Let's figure that your video is going to weigh in somewhere around 30 Megabytes per second. A CD-ROM would be able to hold less than half a minute at this rate, and couldn't even come close to playing it back. The audio alone would gag all but the most robust Internet connections. Figure that the vast majority of the Internet world is still using 56.6K modems. Without compression it would take them more than a week to download the 160 Gigabytes of your movie!

The key to presenting your video/movie over the Web is a subtle balance between compression and bandwidth. Just because you may or may not have big pipes is no indication of what your potential market is dealing with. If your audience does not have a cable modem, ISDN, DSL, or faster, virtually any methodology that you use will present your movie in a tiny window, with limited color-space and haltingly bad synchronization.

One of the best online tutorials for preparing your video for the Internet can be found at (www.iCanStream.com). This joint venture between Media100, Digital Origin, Canon, DigitalFridge, and others, takes you through the operation in a methodical, step-by-step process. For a good, reliable commercial venture that can not only guide you through the capture-edit-stream conga line, but also help you set up your system, check out my good friend Ron Margolis at (www.webvideoguys.com). While you're there check out the *Videoguys' Streaming Video Handbook for Webmasters.*

THE HOLY TRINITY OF STREAMING

What broadcast entertainment was to the past, streaming content will be to the future.

The two most important trade shows for the technology of transmitted entertainment are the NAB (National Association of Broadcasters) and Streaming Media. While NAB has traditionally represented the bastion of time-honored methodology, this year at NAB virtually every booth was showing some sort of streaming adaptation. The Streaming Media East show was perhaps half the size of the Streaming Media West show just a few months later. The incredible growth in this industry segment is a cogent indication of the not-too-distant future.

If you want your movie to be accessible to the widest possible audience, you'll need to offer it in a couple of bandwidth choices on at least two of the three main player formats. A critically important factor to keep in mind is that the four leading OS/computer platforms (PC, Mac, SGI, LINUX) all have very different gamma settings. What appears well balanced on a Windows machine is blown out on a Mac. Inversely, a well-lit and balanced shot on a Mac is so dark on a Windows machine that it is barely recognizable.

Then there are the always important data rate issues. Let's figure for reference purposes that a decent 4 x CD-ROM is good for a sustained data rate of around 400Kbps. Really good compression management can potentially give you about 48 minutes of marginal quality 640 x 480 video. A 56.6 modem is generally good for only 4Kbps, and even the industrial strength T-1 connection is generally dependable for only 20Kbps.

You must be prepared to do battle with the compression gods. The more you understand the potential pitfalls and tricks of streaming media, the brighter your future becomes. Sure, the Internet's bandwidth will increase with time, but the people who have the best compression strategies will always lead the way.

The first step in developing your particular battle plan is deciding on which player technology you want to deal with. Your main choices are QuickTime, RealPlayer and the Windows Media Player.

QuickTime (www.apple.com/quicktime/)

Apple's QuickTime software has more installed users than any other compressed video format. Initially released as part of the

The "Plane Jane" of players also packs the most versatility.

Macintosh operating system, QuickTime is now an integral part of most contemporary browsers. The playback is by far the smoothest of the three players listed here, and its ability to translate and share data between dissimilar platforms has made it an industry standard. QuickTime's wide-ranging acceptance and ease of use make this the optimum distribution mechanism for the vast majority of general Internet uses. It has built-in translators that support more than 200 different file formats and it is particularly well suited to high-quality streaming.

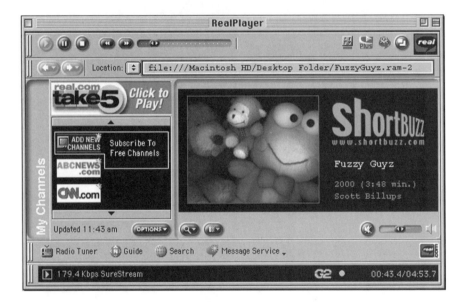

Kinda hard to figure out what does what in the RealPlayer's cluttered environment.

RealPlayer (www.real.com)

Originally developed as a player for the emerging Web-audio market, the RealPlayer is the most popular streaming standard in the PC market, and still leading the way as the codec of choice for a majority of sites. Not nearly as convenient or simple to use as the widely accepted QuickTime, Real does have a few advantages when embedding the data stream into HTML. The picture quality is quite good at high speeds, but the frame rate is quite sensitive to bandpass fluctuations and has a tendency to become choppy. When it's good, it's very good.

While simplicity generally indicates superior engineering, the case of the Windows Media Player is an unfortunate exception.

Windows Media Player (www.microsoft.com/wmp)

This is the streamable version of the popular AVI extension. Despite the fact that it comes from the world's leading software empire, the Windows Media Player has a rather disappointing reputation. Although it is available on both Mac and Windows platforms, the integration with Web browsers is poorly initiated.

WMP's scalable window can occasionally deliver full-screen video streams with near MPEG1 quality if you have the bandwidth. Key word: occasionally. On those rare occasions when the bandwidth gods are smiling down upon you, the Windows Media Player can actually deliver inherent image quality noticeably superior to either QuickTime or RealPlayer.

In their defense, it's really hard to write this kind of application without stepping on someone's intellectual property, and we all know how many people are out gunning for Microsoft. These guys are long overdue for a killer app. Hopefully it will be a robust Web application.

While the MediaCleaner software can create consummately optimized data packages for these and many more compression scenarios, QuickTime is perhaps the codec of choice for many content creators. Ancillary applications such as MacroMedia's Flash and Shockwave are enjoying great success on the Web, and are inherently more compatible within QuickTime's comprehensive architecture.

Since streaming video often requires a special server, hosting services have become the favored means of distribution. They'll generally cater to one of the three flavors of players and can compress your movie for you, or allow you to download it through their FTP site.

A good road stop on your journey through the maze of ambiguity that surrounds this esoteric realm is (www.streamingmediaworld.com). If you've got an itch to be on the leading edge of technogogic hipness, delve into the zippy world of Macromedia's Flash to pump up the graphic artist in your soul. Or savor the soothing richness of Java scripting.

As with all decisions in the moviemaking process, test, tinker and try everything before you crush your movie down to byte-sized chunks.

ON THE OTHER HAND

While streaming most definitely represents the future of media delivery, it does have its drawbacks. Most importantly, it's nearly impossible to save a streamed movie to disk. The paranoid and short-sighted see this as a way to protect their precious intellectual property. The reality is that it severely limits the audience-building potential of your movie.

The Net's economy is entirely different from the corporatized democracy in which we live our physical lives. In the interconnected and reciprocating world of the Internet, the more you give away, the richer you become. When you give your QuickTime away, you're capturing attention. Every time someone e-mails your movie to an associate or shows it to a friend, you're compounding the attention that you and your project receive. To quote Kevin Kelly once more, "The only factor becoming scarce in a world of abundance is human attention. Giving stuff away captures human attention, or mind share, which then leads to market share."

Due to its close proximity to the observer, the relative viewing size of this PCM-CIA video monitor card far exceeds the average home television's perceived size. Movies can be downloaded onto the card directly from the Internet via the PCMCIA port found on most laptop computers or via the tiny RAM card which holds more than 30 minutes of Sorensen compressed, QuickTime video.

Micro-movie venues are about to cascade down from technological heaven. They'll eventually be integrated into just about everything you can imagine. A brisk walk up the Ginza will take you past hundreds of people walking to work, shopping or just leaning up against a building. In their hands are a wide assortment of micro-miniaturized portable venues. Phones playing streaming video on diminutive screens, ultra-tiny LCD panels playing movies from postage-stamp-sized RAM cards.

The chasm between the theater screen and the hand-held device is a big one. Each environment requires certain production considerations, but neither can become exclusionary of the other. Kind of interesting really, how even if you're shooting a multi-million-dollar movie, the original shot is seen on a tiny screen within the camera's viewfinder.

Micro-screens, head-mounted displays and corneal refracting devices are all coming soon to a Circuit City near you. In a way, the coming trend of "handhelds" is perhaps the most intimate and personal venue yet. Until the day when the first cyber-squatter jacks into re-runs of "I Love Lucy," we're on a one-way, no-holds-barred, smack-down battle for human attention.

Compression is the key to our digital future, whether used for downlinking a data stream for theatrical release, or bouncing some homespun content off a fan's cornea halfway around the world. Where it all ends up is a matter of conjecture, but I can promise you, it will be a most exhilarating ride.

A

F

Film Directing: Shot by Shot

Visualizing from Concept to Screen

Steven D. Katz

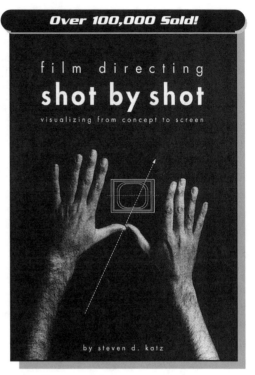

An instant classic since its debut in 1991, "Film Directing: Shot by Shot" and its famous blue cover is one of the most well-known books on directing in the business, and is a favorite of professional directors as an on-set quick reference guide. This international bestseller is packed with visual techniques for filmmakers and screenwriters to expand their stylistic knowledge.

Contains in-depth information on shot composition, staging sequences, previsualization, depth of frame, camera techniques, and much more.

Contains over 750 storyboards and illustrations, including never before published storyboards from Steven Spielberg's *Empire of the Sun*, Orson Welles' *Citizen Kane*, and Alfred Hitchcock's *The Birds*.

> *"(To become a director) you have to teach yourself what makes movies good and what makes them bad. John Singleton has been my mentor…he's the one who told me what movies to watch and to read the book* Shot by Shot.*"*
> **Ice Cube**, Rap artist, actor and filmmaker
> Quoted in *The New York Times*, April 16, 1998

Doubleday Stage & Screen Book Club Selection
Movie Entertainment Book Club Selection

$24.95, ISBN: 0-941188-10-8
370 pages, 7 x 10, 750+ illus.
Order # 7RLS

Both Katz books only $44

Setting Up Your Shots:

Great Camera Moves Every Filmmaker Should Know

Jeremy Vineyard

Whether you need to learn the difference between a jump cut and a match cut or you're a working filmmaker looking for visual ideas on how to best communicate the stories you want to tell, *Setting Up Your Shots* is an encyclopedia of camera moves and cinematic storytelling techniques that directors of all levels will find useful.

Written in clear, non-technical language and laid out in a nonlinear format with self-contained chapters for easy reference, this book provides detailed descriptions of more than 100 camera setups, angles and techniques, using examples from over 140 popular films. An excellent primer for beginning filmmakers, as well as a handy quick-reference guide for experienced directors.

Contains 150 references to the great shots of your favorite films, including *2001: A Space Odyssey, Blue Velvet, Citizen Kane, The Matrix, She's Gotta Have It, The Usual Suspects* and *Vertigo.*

> *"Perfect for any film enthusiast looking for the secrets behind creating film...it is a great addition to the collection of students and film pros alike."*
> **Ross Otterman**
> *Directed By* Magazine

JEREMY VINEYARD is a Los Angeles-based writer, director and software engineer. He has just completed post-production on *The Meridian Project*, a sci-fi short film he wrote and directed. He is also working on an epic fantasy graphic novel series called Paraxis™, which you can learn more about by visiting **www.paraxis.com**.

Doubleday Stage and Screen Selection

$19.95, ISBN 0-941188-73-6
135 pages, 11 x 7, horizontal wide screen format
Order # 8RLS

Directing Actors

Creating Memorable Performances for Film & Television

Judith Weston

The most crucial relationship on a movie set is between the director responsible for the telling of a story and the actors entrusted with bringing that story's characters to life. Good communication between actor and director can mean the difference between a great film and a missed opportunity.

Directing Actors is a method for establishing creative, collaborative relationships between actors and directors that takes the reader on a journey through the complexities of the creative process itself. Using simple, practical tools that both directors and actors can use immediately, this book shows you how to get the most out of rehearsals, troubleshoot poor performances, and give directions that are clear, succinct and easy to follow.

"This is everything a director should know about working with actors."
Steven Charles Jaffe, Executive Producer, *Ghost*; producer, *Star Trek VI*, *Strange Days*

"I think that if Judith's book were mandatory reading for all directors, the quality of the director-actor process would be transformed, and better drama would result."
John Patterson, Director, *The Sopranos, The Practice, Law and Order, Hill Street Blues, Rockford Files*

"Judith's course is probably the single best thing you could do for yourself as a director. I was able to use the

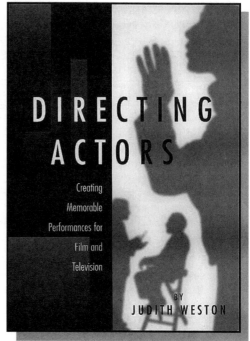

techniques the very next day on the set. Judith has made a difference in my career."
Brian Roberts, Director, *Everybody Loves Raymond, The Drew Carey Show, King of Queens, The Hughleys*

Doubleday Stage & Screen Book Club Selection

JUDITH WESTON draws on 20 years of experience as an actress and teacher of acting. With her seminars, workshops and private consultations, she has helped thousands of actors refine their craft and nearly as many directors clarify their directing and casting choices.

$26.95, ISBN 0-941118-24-8
300 pages, 6 x 9
Order # 4RLS

The Writer's Journey

—2nd Edition

Mythic Structure for Writers

Christopher Vogler

1st Edition - Over 100,000 Sold!

THE WRITER'S JOURNEY
2ND EDITION
MYTHIC STRUCTURE FOR WRITERS

CHRISTOPHER VOGLER

See why this book has become an international best seller, and a true classic. First published in 1992, *The Writer's Journey* explores the powerful relationship between mythology and storytelling in a clear, concise style that's made it required reading for movie executives, screenwriters, scholars, and lovers of pop culture all over the world.

Writers of both fiction and non-fiction will discover a set of useful myth-inspired storytelling paradigms (i.e. *The Hero's Journey*) and step-by-step guidelines to plot and character development. Based on the work of Joseph Campbell, *The Writer's Journey* is a must for writers of all kinds interested in further developing their craft.

The updated and revised 2nd edition provides new insights and observations from Vogler's ongoing work on mythology's influence on stories, movies, and man himself.

> *"This is a book about the stories we write, and perhaps more importantly, the stories we live. It is the most influential work I have yet encountered on the art, nature, and the very purpose of storytelling."*
> **Bruce Joel Rubin**, Screenwriter, *Ghost, Jacob's Ladder*

Book of the Month Club Selection • Writer's Digest Book Club Selection • Movie Entertainment Book Club Selection • Doubleday Stage and Screen Selection

CHRIS VOGLER has been a top Hollywood story consultant and development executive for over 15 years. He has worked on such top grossing feature films as *The Thin Red Line*, *Fight Club*, *The Lion King*, and *Beauty and the Beast*. His international workshops have taken him to Germany, Italy, United Kingdom and Spain, and his literary consulting service Storytech provides in-depth evaluations for professional writers. To learn more, visit his Web site at **www.thewritersjourney.com**.

$22.95, ISBN 0-941188-70-1
300 pages, 6 x 9
Order # 98RLS

The Independent Film and Videomaker's Guide

—2nd Edition
Expanded & Updated

Michael Wiese

This is the new, completely expanded and revised edition with all the information you need from fundraising through distribution. A practical and comprehensive book that will help filmmakers save time and money and inspire them to create successful projects.

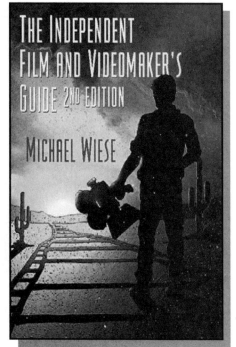

Contents include:

- writing a business plan
- developing your ideas into concepts, treatments and scripts
- directing, producing, market research
- distribution markets (theatrical, home videos, television, international)
- financing your film
- how to do presentations, writing a prospectus
- Plus an appendix filled with film cash flow projections, sample contracts, valuable contact addresses, and much more.

Using the principles outlined in this book, Wiese recently co-directed a 20 minute short film titled "Field of Fish," and is currently developing an independent feature film, *Must Be Love*, to be filmed in England. Additionally, Wiese is national spokesperson for Kodak's Emerging Filmmakers Program. He has conducted his workshops on independent filmmaking in England, Germany, Finland, Indonesia, Ireland, Canada, Australia and throughout the US. Contact Wiese at **mw@mwp.com**.

"The prospectus/business plan (section) of this new edition is alone worth the price of the book."
Release Print, Dec/Jan 1999

"Required reading for anyone serious about making pictures. I recommend

Wiese's book not as a source, but THE source for information regarding independent film and video producing."
Sam L. Grogg
Dean, AFI Center for Advanced Film and Television Studies

"A significant contribution to the literature on independent film production. A "must-read" for anyone seriously interested in independent film."
John Mason
Director of Kodak Worldwide Emerging Filmmaker Program

$29.95, ISBN 0-941188-57-4
500 pages, illustrations, 6 x 9
Order # 37RLS

Storyboarding 101

A Crash Course in Professional Storyboarding

James O. Fraioli

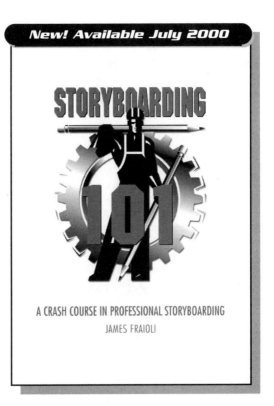

New! Available July 2000

A CRASH COURSE IN PROFESSIONAL STORYBOARDING
JAMES FRAIOLI

If your idea of a dream job is combining your artistic skills with the fast-paced excitement of the entertainment industry, a career as a storyboard artist may be right for you. *Storyboarding 101* is written especially for those looking to break into storyboarding but don't know where to start, with clear and concise information on both the mechanics of the art and how the business works. Artist and filmmaker James O. Fraioli shares his experience as a successful storyboard artist who broke into the business without formal art training, going from security guard to storyboard artist on the set of a major motion picture in a matter of weeks. Topics covered include what storyboards are and why they are necessary, fundamentals of thinking visually, timesaving tricks of the trade, and most importantly, how to land that first job and advance your career.

JAMES O. FRAIOLI began his film career as a storyboard artist on *The Temp*. He has since worked on feature films such as *Wild America*, *Ace Ventura: When Nature Calls* and *Eight Heads In a Duffel Bag*, along with establishing a strong rapport with Walt Disney and Warner Bros. Studios. Visit his Web site at **www.whiteshark.net**.

$19.95, 260 pages, 6 x 9, 75 illustrations
ISBN 0-941188-25-6
Order # 46RLS

Writing the Second Act

Building Conflict and Tension in Your Film Script

Michael Halperin, Ph.D.

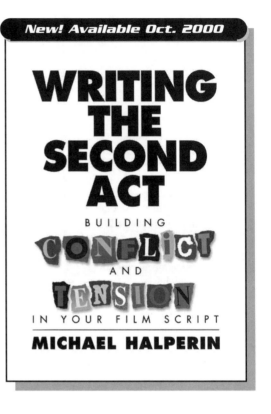

New! Available Oct. 2000

Every screenplay needs an attention-grabbing beginning and a satisfying ending, but those elements are nothing without a strong, well-crafted middle. The second act is where most of the action is: where your characters grow, change, and overcome the obstacles that will bring them to the resolution at the end of the story. Naturally, it's also the hardest act to write, and where most screenplays tend to lose momentum and focus. Author Halperin helps you slay the dragon with *Writing the Second Act*, designed especially for helping screenwriters through that crucial 60-page stretch. Structural elements and plot devices are discussed in detail, as well as how to keep the action moving and the characters evolving while keeping the audience completely absorbed in and entertained by your story.

MICHAEL HALPERIN is a professional writer whose numerous credits include TV shows (*Star Trek: The Next Generation, Quincy*), nonfiction books (*Writing Great Characters*), and interactive media programs (*Voyeur*). He has also worked extensively as a consultant in the television industry, including Executive Story Consultant for 20th Century Fox Television and Creative Consultant on the animated series *Masters of the Universe*. He currently teaches screenwriting at Loyola Marymount University in Los Angeles and is in the process of developing a business-to-business Web site for the entertainment industry.

$19.95, ISBN 0-941188-29-9
240 Pages, 6 x 9
Order # 49RLS

MICHAEL WIESE PRODUCTIONS

11288 Ventura Blvd., Suite 821
Studio City, CA 91604
1-818-379-8799
mwpsales@mwp.com
www.mwp.com

Write or Fax
for a
free catalog.

Please send me the following books:

Title   Order Number (#RLS___)   Amount

_____ _____

_____ _____

_____ _____

_____ _____

SHIPPING   _____

California Tax (8.25%)   _____

TOTAL ENCLOSED _____

Please make check or money order payable to
Michael Wiese Productions

(Check one) ___ Master Card ___ Visa ___ Amex

Credit Card Number_____

Expiration Date_____

Cardholder's Name_____

Cardholder's Signature_____

SHIP TO:

Name_____

Address_____

City_____State_____Zip_____

HOW TO ORDER
CALL
24 HOURS
7 DAYS A WEEK

CREDIT CARD ORDERS CALL
1-800-833-5738

OR FAX YOUR ORDER
818-986-3408

OR MAIL THIS FORM

SHIPPING
ALL ORDERS MUST BE PREPAID
UPS GROUND SERVICE
ONE ITEM - **$3.95**
EACH ADDTNL ITEM, ADD **$2**

EXPRESS - 3 BUSINESS DAYS
ADD **$12** PER ORDER

OVERSEAS
SURFACE - **$15.00** EACH ITEM
AIRMAIL - **$30.00** EACH ITEM

Order online for the lowest prices at
www.mwp.com